PRESENTED TO

....

ON THIS DAY

....

WITH LOVE FROM

....

My First MESSAGE

A DEVOTIONAL BIBLE FOR KIDS

Eugene H. Peterson

Illustrated by Rob Corley and Tom Bancroft

NAVPRESS

Thank you for purchasing a copy of *My First Message*. Now that you are part of *The Message* family we'd love to get to know you better. Visit www.messagebible.com and register to receive updates on future *Message* product releases and valuable discounts.

The Navigators is an international Christian organization. Our mission is to advance the gospel of Jesus and His kingdom into the nations through spiritual generations of laborers living and discipling among the lost. We see a vital movement of the gospel, fueled by prevailing prayer, flowing freely through relational networks and out into the nations where workers for the kingdom are next door to everywhere. NavPress is the publishing ministry of The Navigators. The mission of NavPress is to reach, disciple, and equip people to know Christ and make Him known by publishing life-related materials that are biblically rooted and culturally relevant. Our vision is to stimulate spiritual transformation through every product we publish.

My First Message
Copyright © 2007 by Eugene H. Peterson. All rights reserved.
THE MESSAGE Numbered Edition copyright © 2005.
Copyright © 2007 by FunnyPages Productions, Inc.

www.messagebible.com

Creative Team: Kent Wilson, Scharlotte Rich, Lori Mitchell, Kris Wallen, Arvid Wallen,
Don Simpson, John Blase
Design by studiogearbox.com
Illustrated by Rob Corley and Tom Bancroft. Colors by Jon Conkling.

My First Message
ISBN-10: 1-57683-448-4
ISBN-13: 978-1-57683-448-0

Library of Congress Cataloging-in-Publication Data

Bible. English. Message. 2007.
  My first message : a devotional Bible for kids / Eugene H. Peterson ;
illustrated by Rob Corley and Tom Bancroft ; colors by Jon Conkling. --
1st ed.
    p. cm.
  ISBN 1-57683-448-4
 1. Bible--Devotional use--Juvenile literature. I. Peterson, Eugene H.,
1932- II. Corley, Rob, ill. III. Bancroft, Tom, ill. IV. Title.
BS195.M47 2007b
220.5'209--dc22

                    2006035508

**Published in association with the literary agency of Alive Communications, Inc., 7680 Goddard St.,
Suite 200, Colorado Springs, CO 80920.**

Printed in Japan

2 3 4 5 6 7 8 9 10 / 12 11 10 09 08 07

CONTENTS

INTRODUCTION

Long before the rendition of the Bible known as *The Message* was completed, Eugene Peterson translated portions of the Bible for members of his congregation so they could grasp the powerful relevancy of God's message. Eugene knew the life-changing potential of interacting with the Scriptures. But he also knew that unless people understood what they were reading—by hearing it in a way that connected it to their lives—change wouldn't take place. That is the spirit behind *My First Message*, a children's devotional Bible for kids between the ages of four and eight, their parents, grandparents, and friends.

Why *My First Message* Is Different
Many children's Bibles simplify biblical stories to make them easier for children to understand. But parents have told us that they prefer reading a *real* Bible story rather than a simplified retelling of the story. That's why we've used the text from *The Message* for the fifty Bible stories featured. The Old Testament stories are told in Bible book order, the New Testament stories are chronological. In some cases we've eliminated words or minor parts of the story your child may not understand. We've included whimsical, fun illustrations to further engage your child with the story, trying to be as historically accurate as possible with the details.

My First Message is a devotional Bible for you to use with your children to help them develop a lifelong habit of devotional interaction with God's Word. These devotionals emphasize thinking about what Scripture means and putting it into practice in a way appropriate for children four to eight years old.

Read. Think. Pray. Live.
My First Message uses a time-tested practice of *lectio divina*—or "spiritual reading"— a simple but powerful practice used by Christians for centuries to deepen their

devotional lives. It is based on four key elements: *reading* the Bible, *thinking* about what it means, *praying* in response to what it says, and *living* out the truth.

Read. You want your kids to know that these are *true* stories, but they are still *stories*. Have fun with them. Add inflection to emphasize important points. Use different voices to help your kids differentiate between the characters. Don't worry that you're not good enough at creating voices. Your kids will love it! As you read, encourage your child to look for Manty, the praying mantis character hidden in many of the illustrations.

Think. Almost every page in *My First Message* includes a "Think" question. Some of the questions are intended to convey information ("How much taller than you was Goliath?"). Others put your child in the shoes of the characters ("Why wasn't David afraid of the giant?"). Use the questions as they are written or adapt them to your child's situation. Be sure to pause after each page to ask the "Think" question. Don't be afraid of silence after you ask the question. The goal is not to get easy answers but to stimulate real interaction with Scripture. Feel free to reword the questions—or substitute your own questions that you think are more appropriate for the age of your child.

Pray. This is a chance for your child to interact with God about the things you've read. There are helpful suggestions for tying the readings to your prayer time, but there isn't a written prayer for your child to recite. This is a chance to teach your child that prayer isn't just repeating religious-sounding words—it's an opportunity to talk to God freely and honestly.

Read the "Pray" section aloud to your child. The first time or two through this section you may want to demonstrate to your child how you talk to God. Keep it short and childlike. Encourage your child to insert his or her own thoughts into their conversation with God. Remind your child that it's not about getting it right—it's about talking honestly with God.

Live. The fun activities in each "Live" section help kids see what it means to live out the principles they've just heard, thought about, and prayed about. It's your child's chance to change behavior or start a new pattern of behavior. Don't feel like you have to do all of the activities. Pick the one that you think is most appropriate for your child and have fun with it. If you don't have time for the "Live" activity, don't worry. You can come back to it at a more appropriate time.

How to Effectively Use This Bible with Your Child
Remember that children are kids! You don't want to talk down to them, but don't expect them to have your capacity to absorb information. Here are some suggestions to get the most out of this devotional experience.

Allow about 10–15 minutes for each story. That should be an adequate amount of time to read, think, pray, and do a short, fun application activity. If you don't have time to finish the story, that's okay. The important thing is not the quantity of time you spend—it's the quality of time you spend interacting with God and his Word.

Look for Manty. As you read, encourage your child to look for Manty, the praying mantis character that is hidden in many of the illustrations.

Plan to read only one story at a time. The goal is not to cram as much information as possible into your children's heads—it's to have them understand and interact with smaller chunks of information. Allow them time to absorb the information and internalize it. Make this a fun experience.

Take your time. A good storyteller never rushes the story. You're not trying to finish an activity—you're trying to help your child build a relationship with God. That takes time. Your goal isn't to get through the story to the application. The stories are valuable on their own and if you make reading them a fun experience, your kids will remember them for life.

Enjoy the "fun" elements built into the experience. Your children may be more excited about the illustrations and Manty the praying mantis than about the story. Don't worry! An illustration may be the thing that reminds your child of the truths he or she has been exposed to, even if all the words didn't register.

Prepare yourself. Familiarize yourself with the story, the "Think" sections, and the "Live" activities before you start. Take time to think through the characters (and get your "voices" ready!), think about the prayer time, and have an idea which "Live" activity your child will enjoy.

A Lifetime of Devotion to God's Word

Even though this devotional Bible nudges your children toward acting on the truths they've heard, we've made it accessible and fun. We want your children to keep reading the Bible, thinking about what it means, praying about what they read, and living out the truths they discover daily—for the rest of their lives.

Our hope is that as you and your child read these stories, think about them, pray about them, and live out the truths they contain, you hear your child say:
"This is the most fun Bible I've ever read."
"Can we keep reading?"
"I want to be like David."
"I can trust God too!"

GENESIS
1-2

CREATION
OF HEAVEN AND EARTH

First this: God created the Heavens and Earth—all you see, all you don't see. Earth was a dark soup of nothing, a bottomless emptiness. God's Spirit watched like a bird above the deep, dark water.

God spoke: "Light!" And light appeared.

God saw that light was good.

God named the light Day, he named the dark Night.

It was evening, and it was morning—Day One.

God spoke: "Sky!" And there it was:

he named sky the Heavens;

it was evening, and it was morning—Day Two.

Which do you like better, daytime or nighttime? Why?

God spoke: "Land, appear!" And there it was. God named the land Earth.
He named the pooled water Ocean.
God saw that it was good.

God spoke: "Earth! Grow all varieties of green plants,
        Every sort of fruit tree." And there it was.
        God saw that it was good.
        It was evening, it was morning—Day Three.

God spoke: "Lights! Come out! Shine in Heaven's sky!
        Separate Day from Night." And there it was.
        God made two big lights, the larger to take charge of Day,

the smaller to be in charge of Night;
and he made the stars.
God saw that it was good.
It was evening, it was morning—Day Four.

God spoke: "Ocean, fill with fish and all sea life!
Birds, fly through the sky over Earth!"
God saw that it was good.
God blessed them: "Fish in the waters—have children!
Birds in the sky—have children!"
It was evening, it was morning—Day Five.

If you could create
anything you wanted,
what would it be?

13

God spoke: "Earth! Become alive with every kind of life!"
And there it was: wild animals of every kind,
cattle of all kinds, every sort of reptile and bug.
God saw that it was good.

God spoke: "Let us make people to reflect our image,
so they can take care of the fish in the sea,
the birds in the air, the cattle, and, yes, Earth itself."
God created people in his image, reflecting his nature.
He created them male and female.
God blessed them: "Have children!
Take care of every living thing on the Earth."

Then God said, "I've given you every sort of plant and fruit tree for food.
To everything that moves and breathes
I give whatever grows out of the ground for food." And there it was.

God looked over everything he had made;
it was so good, so very good!
It was evening, it was morning—Day Six.

Is there anyone in your family that you look like?

eaven and Earth were finished, down to the last detail.

By the seventh day God had finished his work.
He rested on the seventh day,
he rested from all his work.

God blessed the seventh day.
He made it a Holy Day
because on that day he rested from his work,
all the creating God had done.

ADAM AND EVE

At the time GOD made Earth and Heaven, GOD formed Man out of dirt from the ground and blew into his nose the breath of life. The Man became alive, a living soul!

When you make something from clay or play dough, why can't you blow on it and make it come alive?

Then GOD planted a garden in Eden. GOD made all kinds of trees grow, trees beautiful to look at and good to eat. The Tree-of-Life was in the middle of the garden, also the Tree-of-Knowing-Good-and-Evil. A river flows out of Eden to water the garden and from there divides into four rivers.

18

PRAY

Sit outside and think about God's creation. Thank God for some of the things he made in the world.

LIVE

Draw a picture or use modeling clay to make something you liked in the Creation story.

Ask your parents if you can stay up one night and watch the moon and stars come out.

GOD took the Man and set him down in the Garden of Eden to work the ground and keep it in order.

GOD commanded the Man, "You can eat from any tree in the garden, except from the Tree-of-Knowing-Good-and-Evil. Don't eat from it. The moment you eat from that tree, you're dead."

GOD said, "It's not good for the Man to be alone; I'll make him a helper, a partner." So GOD formed from the dirt of the ground all the animals of the field and all the birds of the air. He brought them to the Man to see what he would name them. Whatever the Man called each living creature, that was its name. The Man named the cattle, named the birds of the air, named the wild animals; but he didn't find a partner.

GOD put the Man into a deep sleep. As he slept he removed one of his ribs and GOD then used the rib to make Woman and brought her to the Man.

The Man said,
"Finally! My partner!
Name her Woman

for she was made from my flesh and bones."

That's why a man leaves his father and mother and embraces his wife.

They become one flesh.

The two of them, the Man and his Wife, were naked, but they did not

feel ashamed.

PRAY

God gave Adam and Eve rules to obey. What kinds of rules are you supposed to obey at your house or your school? Pray about following the rules this week. Ask God to help you.

LIVE

Draw a picture of the Tree-of-Life and the Tree-of-Knowing-Good-and-Evil.

Plant a garden outside or plant seeds in a cup or pot full of dirt and put it in a sunny window. Take care of it like Adam and Eve took care of the garden.

SiN AND THE FALL

The serpent was clever, more clever than any wild animal GOD had made. He spoke to the Woman: "Do I understand that God told you not to eat from any tree in the garden?"

The Woman said to the serpent, "Not at all. It's only the tree in the middle of the garden that GOD said, 'Don't eat from it; don't even touch it or you'll die.'"

The serpent told the Woman, "You won't die. God knows that the moment you eat from that tree, you'll be just like God, knowing everything from good to evil."

When the Woman saw that the tree looked like good eating and realized she'd know everything, she took and ate the fruit and then gave some to her husband, and he ate.

How did the serpent make disobeying God sound like a good thing to do?

24

Immediately the two of them saw themselves naked! They sewed fig leaves together as makeshift clothes for themselves.

When they heard the sound of GOD strolling in the garden in the evening breeze, the Man and his Wife hid in the trees of the garden, hid from GOD.

GOD called to the Man: "Where are you?"

He said, "I heard you in the garden and I was afraid because I was naked. And I hid."

GOD said, "Who told you you were naked? Did you eat from that tree I told you not to eat from?"

The Man said, "The Woman you gave me as my partner, she gave me fruit from the tree, and, yes, I ate it."

GOD said to the Woman, "What is this that you've done?"

"The serpent tricked me," she said, "and I ate."

$\mathcal{G}$OD told the serpent:

"Because you've done this, you're cursed,
   cursed beyond all cattle and wild animals,
Cursed to slink on your belly
   and eat dirt all your life.
There'll be trouble between you and the Woman,
   between your children and hers.
He'll wound your head,
   you'll wound his heel."
   He told the Woman:
"Now you'll give birth to your babies in pain.
And pleasing your husband
   will be painful too."
   He told the Man:
"Because you listened to your wife
   and ate from the tree
That I commanded you not to eat from,
   'Don't eat from this tree,'
The very ground is cursed because of you;
   getting food from the ground
Will be as painful as having babies is for your wife;
   you'll be working in pain all your life long.
   The ground will sprout thorns and weeds,

Did Eve choose to disobey God, or did the serpent make her?

27

You'll get your food the hard way,
   sweating in the fields,
Until you return to that ground you started
   from, dead and buried."

The Man, known as Adam, named his wife Eve because she was the mother of all the living.

God made leather clothing for Adam and his wife and dressed them.

God said, "The Man has become like one of us, capable of knowing everything from good to evil. What if he now should reach out and take fruit from the Tree-of-Life and eat, and live forever? Never — this cannot happen!"

So God threw them out of the Garden of Eden and sent them to work the ground, the same dirt out of which they'd been made. He stationed angel-cherubim and a revolving sword of fire east of the garden, guarding the path to the Tree-of-Life.

PRAY

List some of the choices that you have to make every day. Ask God to help you to make good choices.

LiVE

Ask your parents to tell you about a time when they made the wrong choice and something bad happened. Next ask them to tell you about a time when they made the right choice and something good happened.

THE FLOOD

This is the story of Noah: Noah was a good man, trusted by his neighbors. Noah walked with God. Noah had three sons: Shem, Ham, and Japheth.

As far as God was concerned, the Earth had become a very bad place; there was violence everywhere.

God said to Noah, "It's all over. The evil is everywhere; I'm making a clean sweep.

What do you think "Noah walked with God" means?

31

"Build yourself a ship from teakwood. Make rooms in it. Make it long, and wide, and high. Build a roof for it and put in a window; put in a door on the side; and make three decks, lower, middle, and upper.

"I'm going to bring a flood on the Earth that will destroy everything alive under Heaven.

"But I'm going to create a **covenant** with you: You'll board the ship, you and your family. Take two of each living creature, a male and a female, so as to save their lives along with yours. Also get all the food you'll need and store it up for you and them."

Noah did everything God commanded him to do.

Next God said to Noah, "Out of everyone alive today, you're different.

"Take clean animals, unclean animals, and every kind of bird. In just seven days I will dump rain on Earth for forty days and forty nights."

Noah did everything God commanded him.

Covenant—*A promise people make to others.*

One day, in the six-hundredth year of Noah's life, the underground springs and the windows of Heaven were thrown open. That's the day Noah and his family boarded the ship. And with them every kind of wild and domestic animal, clean and unclean. They came to Noah and to the ship in pairs. Then GOD shut the door behind them.

The flood continued forty days and the waters rose and lifted the ship high over the Earth. The flood got worse until all the highest mountains were covered. God wiped out every living creature. Only Noah and his company on the ship lived.

What would it be like to live with a zoo full of animals in your room?

Then God caused the wind to blow and the floodwaters began to go down.

In the seventh month, the ship landed on the Ararat mountains. After forty days Noah opened the window. He sent out a dove, but it couldn't find a place to perch. Noah reached out, caught it, and brought it back into the ship.

He waited seven more days and sent out the dove again. It came back in the evening with a freshly picked olive leaf in its beak. Noah knew that the flood was about finished.

In the six-hundred-first year of Noah's life, the flood had dried up. Noah opened the hatch of the ship and saw dry ground.

How do you think Noah felt the first time the dove came back? What about the second time?

God spoke to Noah: "Leave the ship, you and your family. And take all the animals with you so they can have children and live on the Earth. I'm setting up my covenant with you including your children who will come after you, along with everything alive around you. I'm putting my rainbow in the clouds, a sign of the covenant between me and the Earth. From now on, when I form a cloud over the Earth and the rainbow appears in the cloud, I'll remember my covenant between me and you and everything living, that never again will floodwaters destroy all life."

PRAY

Tell God which animals you like the most. Praise him for saving all of the animals for us to enjoy.

LIVE

Go for a walk with your family. Talk about God along the way. As you walk, look for things he made for you to enjoy.

After a rainstorm, look for a rainbow in the sky.

Goats, sheep, and cows butt heads when they are not getting along. What happens when you disagree or "butt heads" with someone in your family?

JACOB AND ESAU

This is the family tree of Isaac son of Abraham: Abraham and Sarah had Isaac. Isaac was forty years old when he married Rebekah. She was the sister of Laban the Aramean.

Isaac prayed hard to GOD for his wife because she could not have children. GOD answered his prayer and Rebekah became pregnant. But the children tumbled and kicked inside her so much that she said, "If this is the way it's going to be, why go on living?" She went to GOD to find out what was going on.

GOD told her,

Two nations are in your belly,

two peoples butting heads while still in your body.

One people will overpower the other,

and the older will serve the younger.

When her time to give birth came, sure enough, there were twins in her belly. The first came out reddish, as if snugly wrapped in a hairy blanket; they named him Esau (Hairy). His brother followed, his fist clutched tight to Esau's heel; they named him Jacob (Heel). Isaac was sixty years old when they were born.

How did God make you special and different from your brother, sister, or friends?

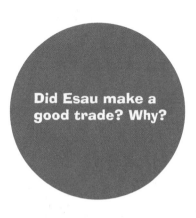

Did Esau make a good trade? Why?

The boys grew up. Esau became an expert hunter, an outdoorsman. Jacob was a quiet man preferring life indoors among the tents. Isaac loved Esau because he loved to eat the animals he hunted, but Rebekah loved Jacob.

One day Jacob was cooking a stew. Esau came in from the field, starved. Esau said to Jacob, "Give me some of that red stew—I'm starved!" That's how he came to be called Edom (Red).

Jacob said, "Make me a trade: my stew for your **rights as the firstborn.**"

Rights as the firstborn—*In biblical times the oldest child was given the family property when the father died (birthright).*

45

Esau said, "I'm starving! What good is a birthright if I'm dead?"

Jacob said, "First, promise me." And he did it. With a promise Esau traded away his rights as the firstborn. Jacob gave him bread and the red stew. He ate and drank, got up and left. That's how Esau shrugged off his rights as the firstborn.

PRAY

Have you had a disagreement with your brother, sister, or friend this week? Confess it to God and ask him to help you get along.

LIVE

How well do you know your family? Play a guessing game with questions like: What is my favorite color? Favorite game? Favorite food? Favorite animal? Favorite place to have fun? Favorite movie?

Make a short list of ways people in your family are the same and ways they are different.

JOSEPH THE DREAMER

When Jacob's son Joseph was seventeen years old, he helped out his brothers in herding the animal flocks. Jacob loved Joseph more than any of his other sons, and he made him a fancy coat. When his brothers realized that their father loved him more than them, they grew to hate Joseph—they wouldn't even speak to him.

Joseph had a dream. When he told it to his brothers, they hated him even more. He said, "Listen to this dream I had. We were all out in the field gathering bundles of wheat. All of a sudden my bundle stood straight up and your bundles circled around it and bowed down to mine."

His brothers said, "So! You're going to rule us? You're going to boss us around?" And they hated him more than ever because of his dreams and the way he talked.

He had another dream and told this one also to his brothers: "I dreamed another dream—the sun and moon and eleven stars bowed down to me!"

Why were Joseph's brothers jealous of him?

49

When he told it to his father and brothers, his father scolded him: "What's with all this dreaming? Am I and your mother and your brothers all supposed to bow down to you?" Now his brothers were really jealous; but his father wondered to himself about the whole business.

Joseph's brothers had gone off to Shechem where they were pasturing their father's flocks. Jacob said to Joseph, "Your brothers are with flocks in Shechem. Come, I want to send you to them."

Joseph said, "I'm ready."

Jacob said, "Go and see how your brothers and the flocks are doing and bring me back a report." He sent him off from the valley of Hebron to Shechem.

The brothers spotted him off in the distance. By the time he got to them they had cooked up a plot to kill him. The brothers were saying, "Here comes that dreamer. Let's kill him and throw him into one of these old wells; we can say that a vicious animal ate him up. We'll see what his dreams amount to."

Reuben, the oldest brother, heard the others talking and stepped in to save Joseph, "We're not going to kill him. No murder. Go ahead and throw him in this well out here in the wild, but don't hurt him." Reuben planned to go back later and get him out and take him back to his father.

When Joseph reached his brothers, they ripped off the fancy coat he was wearing, grabbed him, and threw him into a well. There wasn't any water in the well.

Joseph's dreams made his family angry. Why?

50

Then the brothers sat down to eat their supper. Looking up, they saw a caravan of traders on their way from Gilead, their camels loaded with spices, ointments, and perfumes to sell in Egypt. Judah said, "Brothers, what are we going to get out of killing our brother and concealing the evidence? Let's sell him to the traders, but let's not kill him—he is, after all, our brother, our own flesh and blood." His brothers agreed.

His brothers pulled Joseph out of the well and sold him for twenty pieces of silver to the traders who took Joseph with them down to Egypt.

Later, Reuben came back and went to the well—no Joseph! He ripped his clothes in despair. Beside himself, he went to his brothers. "The boy's gone! What am I going to do!"

Why do you think Reuben planned to go back and help Joseph escape?

The brothers took Joseph's coat, killed a goat, and dipped the coat in the blood. They took the fancy coat back to their father and said, "We found this. Look it over—do you think this is your son's coat?"

Jacob recognized it at once. "My son's coat—a wild animal has eaten him. My Joseph, torn limb from limb!"

Jacob tore his clothes in grief, dressed in rough burlap, and mourned his son a long, long time. His sons and daughters tried to comfort him, but he refused their comfort. "I'll go to the grave mourning my son." Oh, how his father wept for him.

In Egypt the traders sold Joseph to Potiphar, one of Pharaoh's officials, manager of his household affairs.

PRAY

Being thankful for what we have is a good way to keep from being jealous or wanting things others have. Do you have anything special you can thank God for?

LIVE

See how long a list you can make of things you are thankful for. Write it or draw pictures. List some things that can't be bought in a store.

Memorize
2 Thessalonians 1:3:
It's only right that we give thanks.

JOSEPH
AND THE FAMINE (PART 1)

GENESIS 42-43

The land of Canaan was hit hard by famine. Ten of Joseph's brothers went down to Egypt to get food, but Jacob didn't send Benjamin with them; he was afraid that something bad might happen to him.

Joseph was running the country, giving out food to all the people. When Joseph's brothers arrived, he said, "Where do you come from?"

"From Canaan," they said. "We've come to buy food."

Joseph knew who they were, but they didn't know who he was.

Joseph, remembering the dreams he had dreamed of them, said, "You're spies."

"No, we've only come to buy food."

He said, "No. You're spies."

They said, "There were twelve of us brothers—sons of the same father in the country of Canaan. The youngest is with our father, and one is no more."

But Joseph said, "This is how I'll test you. You're not going to leave this place until your younger brother comes here."

Then he threw them into jail for three days.

Why do you think Joseph didn't tell his brothers who he really was?

How do you think Joseph felt when he saw his brothers again? Had he forgiven them for selling him?

On the third day, Joseph spoke to them. "Do this and you'll live. I'm a God-fearing man. If you're as honest as you say you are, one of your brothers will stay here in jail while the rest of you take the food back to your hungry families. Bring your youngest brother back to me and not one of you will die." They agreed.

Joseph took Simeon and made a prisoner of him.

Then Joseph ordered that their sacks be filled with grain, that their money be put back in each sack, and that they be given food for the road. That was all done for them.

They loaded their food supplies on their donkeys and set off.

That night, one of them opened his sack. He called out to his brothers, "My money has been returned!"

They were puzzled—and frightened. "What's God doing to us?"

When they got back to their father Jacob, back in the land of Canaan, they told him everything that had happened.

As they were emptying their food sacks, each man found his purse of money. Their father said to them, "Joseph's gone, Simeon's gone, and now you want to take Benjamin. My son will not go. He is all I have left."

The famine got worse. Their father said, "Go back and get some more food."

But Judah said, "If you're ready to release Benjamin, we'll go. But if you're not, we aren't going."

Their father Israel gave in. "But do this: stuff your packs with gifts. And pay back double what was returned to your sacks. And may The Strong God give you grace in that man's eyes."

The men took the gifts, double the money, and Benjamin. When Joseph saw that they had Benjamin with them, he told his servant, "Take these men; make them feel at home."
But they became anxious, thinking, "He thinks we ran off with the money."

So they went up to Joseph's servant and said, "We came down here one other time to buy food. On our way home, we opened our bags and found our money. We've brought it all back. We have no idea who put the money in our bags."

What were Joseph's brothers afraid of?

The servant said, "Don't worry. Your God and the God of your father has blessed you." And he presented Simeon to them.

When Joseph got home, they presented him with the gifts.

Joseph welcomed them and said, "And your old father whom you mentioned to me, how is he? Is he still alive?"

They said, "Yes—your servant our father is quite well, very much alive."

Then Joseph picked out his brother Benjamin.

Deeply moved on seeing his brother, Joseph hurried out into another room and cried. Then he washed his face, and said, "Let's eat."

And so the brothers feasted with Joseph.

PRAY

Thank God for each person in your family. Is there anything special you'd like to say about each one?

LIVE

Talk about what makes a family. How does each person make your family special? Is someone very good at sharing, cooking, drawing, loving, tickling, helping, or having fun?

JOSEPH

AND THE FAMINE (PART 2)

Joseph ordered his servant: "Fill the men's bags with food and replace each one's money. Then put my chalice, my silver chalice, in the top of the bag of the youngest."

They were barely out of the city when Joseph said to his servant, "Run after them. When you catch up with them, say, 'Why did you steal from me? This is the chalice my master drinks from!'"

He caught up with them and repeated all this word for word.

They said, "We would never do anything like that!"

The servant searched their bags, going from oldest to youngest. The chalice showed up in Benjamin's bag.

They ripped their clothes in sadness and went back to the city.

Why did Joseph order his servant to give the money back and hide the silver chalice in his brother's bag?

Joseph was still at home when his brothers got back. They threw themselves down on the ground in front of him.

Joseph accused them: "How can you have done this?"

Judah said, "What can we say, master? We're all as guilty as the one with the chalice."

"I'd never do that to you," said Joseph. "Only the one will be my slave. The rest of you are free to go back to your father."

Judah came forward. He said, "You asked us, 'Do you have a father and a brother?' And we answered honestly, 'We have a father who is old and a younger brother. His brother is dead and he is the only son left from that mother. And his father loves him more than anything.'

"Then you told us, 'Bring him down here so I can see him or you won't be allowed to see me.'

"When we returned to our father, we told him everything. So when our father said, 'Go back and buy some more food,' we told him, 'We can't; not without our youngest brother.'

"Your servant, my father, told us, 'If you now go and take this one and something bad happens to him, you'll put my old gray, grieving head in the grave for sure.'

"And now, can't you see that if I show up without the boy, this son he loves, he'll die on the spot?

"So let me stay here as your slave. Let the boy go back with his brothers. Oh, don't make me go back and watch my father die in grief!"

Why did Judah offer to become a slave in his brother's place?

Joseph couldn't stand it any longer. He cried out to his brothers: "I am Joseph. Is my father really still alive?" But his brothers were speechless.

"Come closer to me. I am Joseph your brother whom you sold into Egypt. But don't feel badly, don't blame yourselves for selling me. God was behind it. There has been a famine in the land now for two years; the famine will continue for five more years. God sent me on ahead to save your lives. So you see, it wasn't you who sent me here but God.

"Hurry back to my father. Tell him, 'Your son Joseph says: I'm master of all of Egypt. Come as fast as you can. I'll give you a place to live in Goshen where you'll be close to me. I'll take care of you there completely.'"

Then Joseph threw himself on his brother Benjamin's neck and wept, and Benjamin wept on his neck. He then kissed all his brothers and wept over them.

How did Joseph's brothers feel after Joseph told them who he was?

Joseph's brothers left Egypt and went back to their father Jacob in Canaan. When they told him, "Joseph is still alive—and he's the ruler over the whole land of Egypt!" he couldn't believe his ears. But the more they talked, the blood started to flow again—their father Jacob's spirit revived. Israel said, "I've heard enough—my son Joseph is still alive. I've got to go and see him before I die."

PRAY

Talk to God about anything
that's hard or difficult for you
right now. Ask God to make
something good come out of it.

LIVE

Ask your mom or dad if they can think
of times when God took something bad and
turned it into good.

Play a game of "Hide the cup" with a plastic cup.
Have one person go out of the room. Another
person hides the cup. They come back in
and look for it. Family members can tell
them if they are hot (close) or
cold (not close).

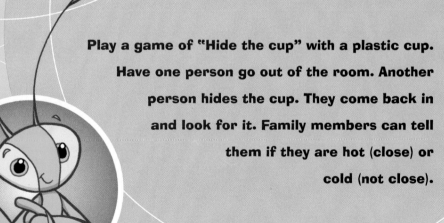

MOSES is BORN

Joseph died, and all his brothers. But the children of Israel kept on having children.

A new king came to power in Egypt who didn't know Joseph. He warned his people, "There are way too many of these Israelites. Let's devise a plan to contain them, because if there's a war they might join our enemies, or just walk off and leave us."

So they put them to work. They built cities for Pharaoh. But the harder the Egyptians worked them the more children the Israelites had—children everywhere! The Egyptians got so they couldn't stand the Israelites and treated them worse than ever.

The Israelites were slaves to the Egyptians. What does that mean?

73

The king of Egypt had a talk with the two Hebrew midwives. He said, "When the Hebrew women deliver a boy, kill him; if it's a girl, let her live."

But the midwives respected God and didn't do what the king of Egypt ordered. The king of Egypt called in the midwives. "Why didn't you obey my orders?"

The midwives answered Pharaoh, "The Hebrew women have their babies before the midwife can get there."

God was pleased with the midwives. And God gave them families of their own.

So Pharaoh commanded all his people: "Every boy that is born, drown him in the Nile. But let the girls live."

Why did the
midwives obey
God and not
Pharaoh?

A man from the family of Levi married a Levite woman. The woman had a son. She saw there was something special about him and hid him for three months. When she couldn't hide him any longer, she got a little basket-boat, placed the child in it, and set it afloat in the reeds at the edge of the Nile.

The baby's older sister watched from a distance to see what would happen to him. Pharaoh's daughter came down to the Nile to bathe. She saw the basket-boat, opened it, and saw the child—a baby crying! She said, "This must be one of the Hebrew babies."

Imagine yourself floating in a basket-boat. What would that feel like?

Then his sister ran up: "Do you want me to get a nursing mother from the Hebrews for you?"

Pharaoh's daughter said, "Yes." The girl went and called the child's mother.

Pharaoh's daughter told her, "Take this baby and nurse him for me. I'll pay you."

After the child was weaned, she presented him to Pharaoh's daughter who adopted him as her son. She named him Moses (which means Pulled-Out) saying, "I pulled him out of the water."

PRAY

Talk to God about how you can be a helper in your home and other places.

LIVE

Think of two things you can do to help someone younger than you and do them this week.

Collect several things that a basket-boat could be made from (such as straw, grass, sticks) and see if you can get them to float in water.

MOSES
AND THE BURNING BUSH

Moses was shepherding and came to the mountain of God, Horeb. The angel of GOD appeared to him in flames of fire blazing out of the middle of a bush. The bush was blazing away but it didn't burn up.

Moses said, "What's going on here? Why doesn't the bush burn up?"

God called to him from out of the bush, "Moses! Moses!"

He said, "Yes? I'm right here!"

God said, "Remove your sandals from your feet. You're standing on holy ground."

A burning bush got Moses' attention. What could God do today that would get your attention?

Then he said, "I am the God of your father: The God of Abraham, the God of Isaac, the God of Jacob."

GOD said, "I've heard the cries of my people in Egypt. And now I have come to get them and bring them to a good land.

"I've seen for myself how cruelly they're being treated by the Egyptians. I'm sending you to Pharaoh to bring my people, the People of Israel, out of Egypt."

Moses answered God, "What makes you think that I could ever lead the children of Israel out of Egypt?"

"I'll be with you," God said.

Then Moses said to God, "Suppose I go to the People of Israel and I tell them, 'The God of your fathers sent me to you'; and they ask me, 'What is his name?'"

God said to Moses, "I-AM-WHO-I-AM. Tell the People of Israel, 'I-AM sent me to you.'

"Now gather the leaders of Israel. Tell them everything I've told you.

"Then you and the leaders of Israel will go to the king of Egypt and say to him: 'Let us take a three-day journey into the wilderness where we will worship GOD—*our* God.'

"The king of Egypt won't let you go easily, so I'll step in with my miracles."

What would it be like to spend three days in the wilderness?

83

Moses objected, "They won't trust me. They won't listen to a word I say."

So GOD said, "What's that in your hand?"

"A staff."

"Throw it on the ground." He threw it. It became a snake!

GOD said to Moses, "Reach out and grab it by the tail." He reached out and grabbed it—and he was holding his staff again.

GOD then said, "Put your hand inside your shirt." He slipped his hand under his shirt, then took it out. The skin of his hand had turned sick.

He said, "Put your hand back under your shirt." He did it, then took it back out—as healthy as before.

"If they aren't convinced by the first and second sign, take some water out of the Nile and pour it out on the dry land; the Nile water will turn to blood when it hits the ground."

Why did Moses say he couldn't obey God and go to Egypt?

Moses raised another objection to GOD: "Master, please, I don't talk well. I stutter."

GOD said, "And who do you think made the human mouth? Isn't it I, GOD? I'll be right there to teach you what to say."

He said, "Oh, Master, please! Send somebody else!"

GOD got angry with Moses: "Don't you have a brother, Aaron the Levite? He speaks very well. You'll speak to him and tell him what to say. I'll be right there with you both, teaching you step by step. Now take this staff in your hand; you'll use it to do the signs."

So Moses returned to Egypt.

PRAY

Think of some things that God wants you to do that are hard to obey. Ask God to help you.

LiVE

Do you always obey your parents and teachers when they ask you to do things or do you disobey sometimes and come up with excuses? How can God help you?

Ask your parents if there are things that they have a hard time obeying. How do they get help from God?

THE PLAGUES

GOD told Moses, "I am going to fill Egypt with miracles, but Pharaoh is not going to listen to you.

"Take your staff and throw it down in front of Pharaoh: It will turn into a snake."

Moses and Aaron did what GOD commanded, and the staff turned into a snake.

Pharaoh called in his magicians, who did the same thing. But then Aaron's staff swallowed their staffs.

Yet Pharaoh wouldn't listen to them.

Why do you think Pharoah would not listen to Moses?

God said to Moses: "Go say to Pharaoh, 'God, the God of the Hebrews, says, "Release my people so that they can worship me in the wilderness." I am going to take this staff that I'm holding and strike this Nile River water: The water will turn to blood.'"

Aaron raised his staff and hit the water in the Nile; all the water in the Nile turned into blood.

But the magicians of Egypt did the same thing. Still Pharaoh remained stubborn.

God said to Moses, "Go to Pharaoh and tell him, 'If you refuse to release my people, I'm warning you, I'll hit the whole country with frogs—the Nile will swarm with frogs—they'll come up into your houses, into your bedrooms, and into your beds!'"

What would it be like to have frogs in your bed?

Aaron stretched his staff over the waters of Egypt and a mob of frogs came up and covered the country.

But again the magicians did the same thing.

Pharaoh still wouldn't listen to Moses and Aaron. Just as GOD had said.

GOD said to Moses, "Tell Aaron, 'Take your staff and strike the dust. The dust will turn into gnats all over Egypt.'"

All the dust of the Earth turned into gnats, gnats everywhere in Egypt.

The magicians tried to produce gnats, but this time they couldn't do it.

GOD said to Moses, "Tell Pharaoh, 'If you don't release my people, I'll release swarms of flies on you.'"

And GOD did just that. All over Egypt, the country was ruined by flies.

But Pharaoh once again wouldn't release the people.

GOD said to Moses, "Tell Pharaoh, 'If you refuse to release my people, GOD will strike your farm animals with a severe disease.'"

And the next day GOD did it. All the farm animals of Egypt died, but not one animal of the Israelites died. But Pharaoh stayed stubborn. He wouldn't release the people.

What does it mean to be stubborn?

GOD said to Moses and Aaron, "Take fistfuls of soot from a furnace and throw it into the air right before Pharaoh's eyes; it will become fine dust all over Egypt and cause sores on people and animals throughout Egypt." So they took soot from a furnace and threw it up into the air. It caused sores on people and animals.

Pharaoh still wouldn't listen.

GOD said to Moses, "Tell Pharaoh, 'This time I am going to strike you with a terrific hailstorm.'"

Moses lifted his staff to the skies and GOD sent peals of thunder and hail shot through with lightning strikes. GOD rained hail down on the land of Egypt. Except for Goshen where the Israelites lived; there was no hail in Goshen.

But when Pharaoh saw that the rain and hail and thunder had stopped, he kept right on sinning, stubborn as ever. He refused to release the Israelites.

Moses and Aaron went to Pharaoh and said to him, "GOD, the God of the Hebrews, says, 'How long are you going to refuse to release my people? Watch out; tomorrow I'm bringing locusts into your country. They'll devour everything left over from the hailstorm, even the saplings out in the fields.'"

Would you change your mind if all these things were happening to you? Why or why not?

Moses stretched out his staff over the land of Egypt.

There never was an invasion of locusts like it in the past, and never will be again.

But Pharaoh still didn't release the Israelites.

GOD said to Moses: "Stretch your hand to the skies. Let darkness descend on the land of Egypt."

Moses stretched out his hand to the skies. Thick darkness descended on the land of Egypt for three days. Nobody could see anybody. Except for the Israelites: they had light where they were living.

But GOD kept Pharaoh stubborn as ever. He wouldn't agree to release them.

PRAY

The opposite of stubborn can be obedient. Pray about ways to obey this week.

LIVE

Look up "stubborn" in the dictionary. Discuss with your family when it is good to listen and be obedient. Now think of times when it is good to be stubborn.

THE FIRST PASSOVER

GOD said to Moses: "I'm going to hit Pharaoh and Egypt one final time, and then he'll let you go."

Then Moses spoke to Pharaoh: "GOD'S Message: 'At midnight I will go through Egypt and every firstborn child in Egypt will die. Also the firstborn of animals.'

"Then all these servants of yours will beg me to leave, 'Leave! You and all the people who follow you!' And I will most certainly leave."

How could Pharaoh have saved his people?

99

GOD said to Moses and Aaron, "Tell all the people of Israel that each man is to take a lamb for his family. Your lamb must be a healthy male, one year old. Then kill it and take some of the blood and smear it on the two doorposts and the frame above the door of the houses in which you will eat it. You are to eat the meat, roasted in the fire, along with bread, made without yeast, and bitter herbs.

"Eat in a hurry; it's the Passover to GOD.

"I will go through the land of Egypt on this night and strike down every firstborn in the land of Egypt. I am GOD. The blood will serve as a sign on the houses where you live. When I see the blood I will pass over you.

"This will be a day to remember; you will celebrate it as a festival to GOD down through the generations.

"This marks the exact day I brought you out in force from the land of Egypt."

Moses assembled all the leaders of Israel. He said, "Select a lamb for your families and kill the Passover lamb. Smear the blood on the frame and on the two doorposts. No one is to leave the house until morning. GOD will pass through to strike Egypt down. When he sees the blood on the frame and the two doorposts, GOD will pass over the doorway.

Why did God tell the Israelites to put blood over the doors and not mud or something else?

"When you enter the land which GOD will give you as he promised, keep doing this. And when your children say to you, 'Why are we doing this?' tell them: 'It's the Passover-sacrifice to GOD who passed over the homes of the Israelites in Egypt when he hit Egypt with death but rescued us.'"

The people bowed and worshiped.

PRAY

Thank God for some of the special ways he takes care of you and your family.

LIVE

Create a way to remember the good things God does. Some families write down things they want to remember and keep them in a decorated box or jar. Then they read them every Thanksgiving.

Some people decorate and keep their own box and read from it on their birthday. They call it their "blessing box."

Why did the king of Egypt want the Israelites to return?

MOSES PARTS THE RED SEA

GOD spoke to Moses: "Tell the Israelites to turn around and camp on the shore of the sea.

"Then I'll make Pharaoh's heart stubborn again and he'll chase after them. And I'll use Pharaoh and his army to put my Glory on display. Then the Egyptians will realize that I am GOD."

And that's what happened.

When the king of Egypt was told that the people were gone, he and his servants changed their minds. They said, "What have we done, letting Israel, our slave labor, go free?" So he had his chariots harnessed up and got his army together.

The Egyptians gave chase and caught up with them where they had made camp by the sea.

105

As Pharaoh approached, the Israelites looked up and saw them—Egyptians! Coming at them!

They were totally afraid. They cried out in terror to God.

Moses spoke to the people: "Don't be afraid. Stand firm and watch God do his work of salvation for you today. God will fight the battle for you."

God said to Moses: "Hold your staff high and stretch your hand out over the sea: Split the sea! The Israelites will walk through the sea on dry ground.

"Meanwhile I'll make sure the Egyptians keep up their stubborn chase."

Then Moses stretched out his hand over the sea and God, with a terrific east wind all night long, made the sea go back. He made the sea dry ground. The seawaters split.

If you were Moses and God told you to make the sea split, how would you do it?

The Israelites walked through the sea on dry ground with the waters a wall to the right and to the left. The Egyptians came after them in full pursuit, every horse and chariot and driver of Pharaoh racing into the middle of the sea. God looked down on the Egyptian army and threw them into a panic. He clogged the wheels of their chariots; they were stuck in the mud.

The Egyptians said, "Run from Israel! God is fighting on their side and against Egypt!"

Gᴏᴅ said to Moses, "Stretch out your hand over the sea and the waters will come back over the Egyptians, over their chariots, over their horsemen."

Moses stretched his hand out over the sea: As the day broke and the Egyptians were running, the sea returned to its place as before. Not one of them survived.

Gᴏᴅ delivered Israel that day from the Egyptians. The people were speechless before Gᴏᴅ and trusted in Gᴏᴅ and his servant Moses.

PRAY

Can you think of a time your family was in trouble? How did God protect you? Say a prayer to God thanking him for keeping you safe.

LIVE

Ask your parents and grandparents to tell you about a time when they had to say yes or no to God. What happened?

For a fun dessert, make a Red Sea of Jell-O in a pan. Part the "waves" and let play figures walk between them.

SINAI AND THE TEN COMMANDMENTS

Three months after leaving Egypt the Israelites entered the Wilderness of Sinai. Israel camped there facing the mountain.

As Moses went up to meet God, GOD called down to him from the mountain: "Tell the People of Israel: 'You have seen what I did to Egypt and how I carried you on eagles' wings and brought you to me. If you will listen obediently to what I say and keep my covenant, out of all peoples you'll be my special treasure.'"

What was God's promise to the Israelites if they kept his rules?

Moses came back and gave them all these words which God had commanded him.

The people all agreed: "Everything God says, we will do." Moses took the people's answer back to God. God said to Moses, "Get ready. I'm about to come to you in a thick cloud so that the people can listen in and trust you completely when I speak with you. Post warnings for the people all around, telling them, 'Warning! Don't climb the mountain. Whoever touches the mountain dies.'"

Then Moses prepared the people for the holy meeting. On the third day at daybreak, there were loud claps of thunder, flashes of lightning, a thick cloud covering the mountain, and an ear-piercing trumpet blast. Everyone in the camp shuddered in fear.

Moses led the people out of the camp to meet God. They stood at attention at the base of the mountain.

Mount Sinai was all smoke because God had come down on it as fire. God descended to the peak of Mount Sinai. God called Moses up to the peak and Moses climbed up.

How would you have felt being so close to God on the mountain?

So Moses went down to the people. He said to them: God spoke all these words:

I am God, your God, who brought you out of the land of Egypt, out of a life of slavery.

No other gods, only me.

No carved gods of any size, shape, or form of anything whatever, whether of things that fly or walk or swim. *I* am God, your God, and I'm a most jealous God.

No using the name of God, your God, in curses or silly talk; God's name is holy.

Work six days and do everything you need to do. But the seventh day is a Sabbath to God, your God. Don't do any work. For in six days God made Heaven, Earth, and Sea, and everything in them; he rested on the seventh day.

Honor your father and mother so that you'll live a long time in the land that God, your God, is giving you.

No murder.

No adultery.

No stealing.

No lies about your neighbor.

No dreaming about your neighbor's house—or anything that is your neighbor's.

All the people, experiencing the thunder and lightning, the
trumpet blast and the smoking mountain, were afraid.

Moses spoke to the people: "Don't be afraid. God has come to
plant a deep respect within you so that you won't sin."

PRAY

Talk to God about rules that are hard for you to obey. Remember that behind every rule is a reason.

LIVE

What would the world be like if there were no people who believed in God and no one followed God's rules of right and wrong? What would your town be like? What would your home be like?

Play your favorite family game. Then try playing it with no rules or have everyone make up their own rules.

JOSHUA
6

THE BATTLE
OF JERICHO

Ark—*A sacred, gold-covered chest containing the Ten Commandments, Aaron's staff, and a jar of the manna that God fed the Israelites while in the wilderness.*

Jericho was shut up tight as a drum because of the People of Israel: no one going in, no one coming out.

God spoke to Joshua, "I've already given Jericho to you, along with its king and its soldiers. Here's what you are to do: March around the city, all your soldiers. Circle the city once. Repeat this for six days. Have seven priests carry seven ram's horn trumpets in front of the **Ark**. On the seventh day march around the city seven times, the priests blowing away on the trumpets. And then, a long blast on the ram's horn—when you hear that, all the people are to shout at the top of their lungs. The city wall will collapse at once."

120

How many of God's instructions to Joshua can you remember?

So Joshua son of Nun called the priests and told them, "Take up the Ark of the Covenant. Seven priests are to carry seven ram's horn trumpets leading God's Ark."

Then he told the people, "Set out! March around the city. Have the armed guard march before the Ark of God."

He sent the Ark of God on its way around the city. It circled once, came back to camp, and stayed for the night.

On the second day they again circled the city once and returned to camp. They did this six days.

What might have happened if Joshua and the Israelites hadn't followed all of God's instructions?

When the seventh day came, they got up early and marched around the city this same way but seven times—yes, this day they circled the city seven times. On the seventh time around, the priests blew the trumpets and Joshua signaled the people, "Shout!—God has given you the city!"

The priests blew the trumpets.

When the people heard the blast of the trumpets, they gave a thunderclap shout. The wall fell at once. The people rushed straight into the city and took it.

God was with Joshua. He became famous all over the land.

PRAY

Thank God for giving us instructions. Ask God to help you with the ones that are the hardest for you to do.

LIVE

Gather some friends, and walk around your house seven times.

Build a pretend Jericho out of Legos or blocks and then shout to God and crash it down.

SAMUEL HEARS GOD SPEAK

The boy Samuel was serving GOD in the temple under Eli's direction. This was at a time when GOD was rarely heard or seen. One night Eli was sound asleep. Samuel was still in bed in the Temple of GOD, where the Ark of God rested.

Then GOD called out, "Samuel, Samuel!"

Samuel answered, "Yes? I'm here." Then he ran to Eli saying, "I heard you call. Here I am."

Eli said, "I didn't call you. Go back to bed." And so he did.

GOD called again, "Samuel, Samuel!"

Samuel got up and went to Eli, "I heard you call. Here I am."

Again Eli said, "Son, I didn't call you. Go back to bed."

GOD called again, "Samuel!"—the third time! Yet again Samuel got up and went to Eli, "Yes? I heard you call me. Here I am."

126

What might have happened if tired young Samuel had just gone back to sleep?

That's when it dawned on Eli that GOD was calling the boy. So Eli directed Samuel, "Go back and lie down. If the voice calls again, say, 'Speak, GOD. I'm your servant, ready to listen.'" Samuel returned to his bed.

Then GOD came and stood before him exactly as before, calling out, "Samuel! Samuel!"

Samuel answered, "Speak. I'm your servant, ready to listen."

How could reading the Bible be like listening to God?

Samuel grew up. GOD was with him, and Samuel always spoke God's words. Everyone in Israel recognized that Samuel was the real thing—a true prophet of GOD.

PRAY

Are there times you have trouble listening to your parents? Tell God about it, and ask him for help in listening better.

LiVE

Play the listening game. Sit in a circle. Have one person whisper something in the first person's ear. Have each person pass it along the same way. Have the last person tell what they heard. Did everyone listen well?

What is the difference between hearing and listening?

DAVID AND GOLIATH

King Saul and the Israelites spread out their troops ready for battle against the Philistines. The Philistines were on one hill, the Israelites on the opposing hill, with the valley between them.

A giant nearly ten feet tall stepped out from the Philistine line into the open, Goliath from Gath. He had a bronze helmet on his head and was dressed in armor—126 pounds of it! He wore bronze shin guards and carried a bronze sword. His spear was like a fence rail—the spear tip alone weighed over fifteen pounds.

Goliath stood there and called out to the Israelite troops, "Why bother using your whole army? Pick your best fighter and pit him against me. If he gets the upper hand and kills me, the Philistines will all become your slaves. But if I get the upper hand and kill him, you'll all become our slaves and serve us. I challenge the troops of Israel this day. Give me a man. Let us fight it out together!"

When Saul and his troops heard the Philistine's challenge, they were terrified and lost all hope.

How much taller than you was Goliath?

133

Now David was the youngest son of Jesse from Bethlehem in Judah. While his three older brothers went to war with Saul, David went back and forth from attending to Saul to tending his father's sheep in Bethlehem.

One day, Jesse told David his son, "Check in on your brothers to see whether they are getting along all right, and let me know how they're doing."

David arrived at the camp just as the army was moving into battle formation, shouting the war cry. The Philistine champion, Goliath of Gath, stepped out from the front lines of the Philistines, and gave his usual challenge. David heard him.

"Master," said David to King Saul, "don't give up hope. I'm ready to go and fight this Philistine."

Saul answered David, "You can't go and fight this Philistine. You're too young and inexperienced."

David said, "I've been a shepherd, tending sheep for my father. Whenever a lion or bear came and took a lamb from the flock, I'd go after it, knock it down, and rescue the lamb. And I'll do the same to this Philistine pig who is taunting the troops of God-Alive. God, who delivered me from the teeth of the lion and the claws of the bear, will deliver me from this Philistine."

Saul said, "Go. And God help you!"

Why wasn't David afraid of the giant?

David didn't want to use armor to protect himself. What did David think would protect him?

Then Saul outfitted David as a soldier in armor. He put his bronze helmet on his head and belted his sword on him over the armor. David tried to walk but he could hardly budge.

David told Saul, "I can't even move with all this stuff on me. I'm not used to this." And he took it all off.

Then David took his shepherd's staff, selected five smooth stones from the brook, and put them in the pocket of his shepherd's pack, and with his sling in his hand approached Goliath.

"Come on," said the Philistine.

"I'll make roadkill of you for the buzzards. I'll turn you into a tasty morsel for the field mice."

David answered, "You come at me with sword and spear and battle-ax. I come at you in the name of GOD-of-the-Angel-Armies, the God of Israel's troops, whom you curse and mock. This very day GOD is handing you over to me. The whole earth will know that there's an extraordinary GOD in Israel. And everyone gathered here will learn that God doesn't save by means of sword or spear. The battle belongs to GOD—he's handing you to us on a platter!"

That angered the Philistine, and he started toward David. David took off from the front line, running toward the Philistine. David reached into his pocket for a stone, slung it, and hit the Philistine hard in the forehead, embedding the stone deeply. The Philistine crashed, facedown in the dirt.

Then David ran up to the Philistine and stood over him, pulled the giant's sword from its sheath. When the Philistines saw that their great champion was dead, they scattered, running for their lives.

PRAY

Tell God about some of the things you are afraid of. Ask God to be with you whenever you are afraid. Ask him to give you courage to be brave and to stand up for what is right.

LIVE

Act out the story, using scrunched up paper or a foam ball as stones. Take turns acting out each part. Talk about heroes.

What is a hero?
Can you name any heroes?

Memorize Philippians 4:6: Instead of worrying, pray.

1 SAMUEL 18-20

DAVID AND JONATHAN

Jonathan became totally committed to David, his number-one **advocate** and friend.

Jonathan, out of his deep love for David, made a covenant with him. He celebrated it with important gifts: his own royal robe and weapons—armor, sword, bow, and belt.

Whatever King Saul gave David to do, he did it—and did it well. Everybody approved of and admired David's leadership.

Advocate—*A friend who helps you when you need it.*

If you gave a gift to someone special, what would you give them?

As they returned home, after David had killed the Philistine, the women poured out of all the villages of Israel singing and dancing,

Saul kills by the thousand,

David by the ten thousand!

This made Saul angry—very angry. He took it as a personal insult. From that moment on, Saul kept his eye on David.

Now Saul feared David. It was clear that GOD was with David and had left Saul. Everything David did turned out well. Yes, GOD was with him.

As Saul more and more realized that GOD was with David, his fear of David increased and settled into hate. Saul hated David. David went to Jonathan. "What have I done to your father that makes him so determined to kill me?

Why did King Saul hate David?

"It's true—as sure as GOD lives, and as sure as you're alive before me right now—he's determined to kill me."

Jonathan said, "Tell me what you have in mind. I'll do anything for you."

David said, "Tomorrow I'm scheduled to eat dinner with the king. Instead, I'll go hide in the field. If your father misses me, say, 'David asked if he could run down to Bethlehem and worship with his family.' If he says, 'Good!' then I'm safe. But if he gets angry, you'll know for sure that he's made up his mind to kill me. If I'm in the wrong, go ahead and kill me yourself."

"Never!" exclaimed Jonathan. "I'd never do that! If I get the slightest hint that my father wants to kill you, I'll tell you."

Jonathan repeated his pledge of love and friendship for David. He loved David more than his own soul!

On the holiday of the New Moon, the king came to the table to eat.

How did Jonathan prove that he was a good friend?

He sat where he always sat, but David's seat was empty.

After day two, David's seat was still empty. Saul asked Jonathan his son, "So where's that son of Jesse? He hasn't eaten with us either yesterday or today."

Jonathan said, "David asked my special permission to go to Bethlehem."

Saul exploded in anger at Jonathan: "Don't you think I know that you're up to something with the son of Jesse? Now go get him. Bring him here. From this moment, he's as good as dead!"

Jonathan stood up to his father. "Why dead? What's he done?"

Saul threw his spear at him to kill him.

That convinced Jonathan that his father was decided on killing David.

In the morning, Jonathan went to the field.

And then they kissed one another and wept, friend over friend, David weeping especially hard.

Jonathan said, "Go in peace! The two of us will be friends in GOD's name forever!"

PRAY

Thank God for your friends.
Ask him to help you be a good
friend in some special way.
Make a new friend by asking God
to show you ways to
be a friend to someone
who needs one.

LiVE

Make a list of your friends and
list the good things about each one.
Then make a list of the things about yourself
that make you a good friend.

Think of a friend you'd like to play with and
ask permission to invite them over
for a play-day.

1 KINGS 18

ELIJAH
AND THE PROPHETS OF BAAL

There was a drought in Israel. The drought was now in its third year. GOD's word came to Elijah. The message: "Go and present yourself to King Ahab; I'm about to make it rain on the country."

The moment Ahab saw Elijah he said, "So it's you, old troublemaker!"

"It's not I who has caused trouble in Israel," said Elijah, "but you—you've dumped GOD's ways and commands and run off after the local gods, the **Baals**. Here's what I want you to do: Assemble everyone in Israel at Mount Carmel. And make sure that the four hundred and fifty prophets of the local gods, the Baals, are there."

So Ahab summoned everyone in Israel, particularly the prophets, to Mount Carmel.

Having no rain for three years was really King Ahab's fault. Why?

Baal—*The name of a false god many unbelievers worshiped.*

Elijah challenged the people: "How long are you going to sit on the fence? If GOD is the real God, follow him; if it's Baal, follow him. Make up your minds!"

Nobody said a word; nobody made a move.

Then Elijah said, "I'm the only prophet of GOD left in Israel; and there are four hundred and fifty prophets of Baal. Let the Baal prophets bring up two oxen; let them pick one, butcher it, and lay it out on an altar on firewood—but don't ignite it. I'll take the other ox, cut it up, and lay it on the wood. But neither will I light the fire. Then you pray to your gods and I'll pray to GOD. The god who answers with fire will prove to be, in fact, God."

All the people agreed: "A good plan—do it!"

Elijah accused the people of sitting on the fence. What does that mean?

Elijah told the Baal prophets, "You go first. Then pray to your god, but don't light the fire."

So they took the ox he had given them, prepared it for the altar, then prayed to Baal. They prayed all morning long, "O Baal, answer us!" But nothing happened—not so much as a whisper of breeze. Desperate, they jumped and stomped on the altar they had made.

By noon, Elijah had started making fun of them, taunting, "Call a little louder—he is a god, after all. You don't suppose he's overslept, do you, and needs to be waked up?" They prayed louder and louder.

This went on until well past noon, but still nothing happened.

Then Elijah told the people, "Enough of that—it's my turn. Gather around." And they gathered. He then put the altar back together, for by now it was in ruins. Then Elijah dug a fairly wide trench around the altar. He laid firewood on the altar, cut up the ox, put it on the wood, and said, "Fill four buckets with water and soak both the ox and the firewood." Then he said, "Do it again," and they did it. Then he said, "Do it a third time," and they did it a third time.

When it was time for the sacrifice to be offered, Elijah the prophet came up and prayed, "O GOD, God of Abraham, Isaac, and Israel, make it known right now that you are God in Israel. Answer me, GOD; O answer me and reveal to this people that you are GOD, the true God."

Immediately the fire of GOD fell and burned up the offering, the wood, the stones, the dirt, and even the water in the trench.

All the people saw it happen and fell on their faces in awed worship, exclaiming, "GOD is the true God! GOD is the true God!"

PRAY

Do you believe God is the one true God like Elijah did? If so, tell him.

LIVE

Look up the word "drought" in the dictionary.

Watch the weather and see when it's going to rain in your neighborhood.

Why was Elijah running away from the wicked queen?

ELIJAH
HEARS A QUIET VOICE

The wicked Queen Jezebel heard that God's prophet Elijah was attempting to turn the people against the false god Baal. Jezebel immediately sent a messenger to Elijah with her threat: "The gods will get you for this and I'll get even with you! By this time tomorrow you'll be dead."

When Elijah saw how things were, he ran for dear life to Beersheba, far in the south of Judah. He then went on into the desert another day's journey. He came to a lone broom bush and collapsed in its shade, wanting in the worst way to be done with it all—to just die: "Enough of this, GOD! Take my life— I'm ready to join my ancestors in the grave!" Exhausted, he fell asleep under the lone broom bush.

Why was Elijah tired and hungry? What did God do to help Elijah?

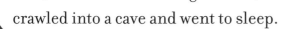

Suddenly an angel shook him awake and said, "Get up and eat!"

He looked around and, to his surprise, right by his head were a loaf of bread baked on some coals and a jug of water. He ate the meal and went back to sleep.

The angel of GOD came back, shook him awake again, and said, "Get up and eat some more—you've got a long journey ahead of you."

He got up, ate and drank his fill, and set out. Nourished by that meal, he walked forty days and nights, all the way to the mountain of God, to Horeb. When he got there, he crawled into a cave and went to sleep.

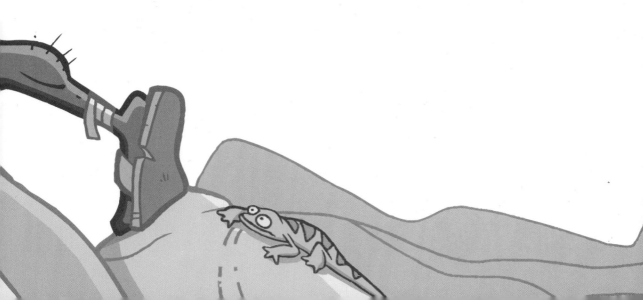

Then the word of GOD came to him: "So Elijah, what are you doing here?"

"I've been working my heart out for the GOD-of-the-Angel-Armies," said Elijah. "The people of Israel have abandoned your covenant, destroyed the places of worship, and murdered your prophets. I'm the only one left, and now they're trying to kill me."

Then he was told, "Go, stand on the mountain at attention before GOD. GOD will pass by."

How did God speak to Elijah? Think of ways God could speak to us.

A hurricane wind ripped through the mountains and shattered the rocks before GOD, but GOD wasn't to be found in the wind; after the wind an earthquake, but GOD wasn't in the earthquake; and after the earthquake fire, but GOD wasn't in the fire; and after the fire a gentle and quiet whisper.

When Elijah heard the quiet voice, he covered his face with his great cloak, went to the mouth of the cave, and stood there. A quiet voice asked, "So Elijah, now tell me, what are you doing

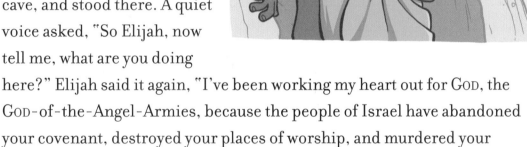

here?" Elijah said it again, "I've been working my heart out for GOD, the GOD-of-the-Angel-Armies, because the people of Israel have abandoned your covenant, destroyed your places of worship, and murdered your prophets. I'm the only one left, and now they're trying to kill me."

GOD said, "Go back the way you came through the desert to Damascus. When you get there anoint several men I will show you, including Elisha to succeed you as prophet. Meanwhile, I'm preserving for myself seven thousand souls: the knees that haven't bowed to the god Baal, the mouths that haven't kissed his image."

Elijah went straight out and found Elisha in a field where there were twelve pairs of yoked oxen at work plowing; Elisha was in charge of the twelfth pair. Elijah went up to him and threw his cloak over him.

Elisha deserted the oxen, ran after Elijah, and said, "Please! Let me kiss my father and mother good-bye—then I'll follow you."

"Go ahead," said Elijah, "but, mind you, don't forget what I've just done to you."

So Elisha left; he took his yoke of oxen and killed them. He made a fire with the plow and tackle and then boiled the meat—a true farewell meal for the family. Then he left and followed Elijah, becoming his right-hand man.

PRAY

Thank God for talking to us through the stories in the Bible. Tell him about stories you especially like. Thank him for always listening to our prayers.

LIVE

Ask your family and other people older than you if they have ever heard God speak to them. Find out what happened.

THE FIERY FURNACE

King Nebuchadnezzar built a gold statue, ninety feet high and nine feet thick. He then ordered all the important leaders in the province, everybody who was anybody, to the dedication ceremony of the statue.

A messenger then proclaimed in a loud voice: "Attention, everyone! Every race, color, and creed, listen! When you hear the band strike up—all the trumpets and trombones, the tubas and baritones, the drums and cymbals—fall to your knees and worship the gold statue that King Nebuchadnezzar has set up. Anyone who does not kneel and worship shall be thrown into a roaring furnace."

The band started to play and everyone fell to their knees and worshiped the gold statue that King Nebuchadnezzar had set up.

Just then, some Babylonian fortunetellers stepped up and said to King Nebuchadnezzar, "Long live the king! You gave strict orders, O king, that whoever did not go to their knees and worship had to be pitched into a roaring furnace. Well, there are some Jews here—Shadrach, Meshach, and Abednego—who are ignoring you, O king. They don't respect your gods and they won't worship the gold statue you set up."

Furious, King Nebuchadnezzar ordered Shadrach, Meshach, and Abednego to be brought in. When the men were brought in, Nebuchadnezzar asked, "Is it true that you don't respect my gods and refuse to worship the gold statue that I have set up? I'm giving you a second chance. If you don't worship it, you will be pitched into a roaring furnace, no questions asked. Who is the god who can rescue you from my power?"

Shadrach, Meshach, and Abednego didn't bow to Nebuchadnezzar. Do you know why?

167

They answered King Nebuchadnezzar, "Your threat means nothing to us. If you throw us in the fire, the God we serve can rescue us from your roaring furnace, O king. But even if he doesn't, it wouldn't make a bit of difference, O king. We still wouldn't serve your gods or worship the gold statue you set up."

Nebuchadnezzar, his face purple with anger, ordered the furnace fired up seven times hotter than usual. He ordered some strong men from the army to tie them up, hands and feet, and throw them into the roaring furnace. Shadrach, Meshach, and Abednego, bound hand and foot, fully dressed from head to toe, were pitched into the roaring fire.

Suddenly King Nebuchadnezzar jumped up in alarm and said, "Didn't we throw three men into the fire?"

"That's right, O king," they said.

"But look!" he said. "I see four men, walking around freely in the fire, completely unharmed! And the fourth man looks like an angel!"

Who was in the fire protecting Shadrach, Meshach, and Abednego?

169

Nebuchadnezzar went to the door of the roaring furnace and called in, "Shadrach, Meshach, and Abednego, servants of the High God, come out here!"

Shadrach, Meshach, and Abednego walked out of the fire.

All the important people, the government leaders and king's counselors, gathered around to examine them and discovered that the fire hadn't so much as touched the three men—not a hair singed, not a scorch mark on their clothes, not even the smell of fire on them!

Nebuchadnezzar said, "Blessed be the God of Shadrach, Meshach, and Abednego! He sent his angel and rescued his servants who trusted in him!"

PRAY

Have you ever felt all alone?
Share your feelings with God.
Read Psalm 139:5: I look
behind me and you're there, then
up ahead and you're there, too—
your reassuring presence,
coming and going.

LIVE

Ask your parents to help you roast
marshmallows over a campfire, grill, or stove
and notice how the marshmallows change.

Close your eyes and imagine how God
protected Shadrach,
Meshach, and Abednego.

DANIEL
IN THE LIONS' DEN

Darius the king reorganized his kingdom. Daniel was so much smarter than the other leaders that the king decided to put him in charge of the whole kingdom.

The other leaders got together to find something in Daniel's life that they could use against him, but they couldn't dig up anything. He was totally trustworthy. So they cooked up a plan and then went to the king and said, "King Darius, live forever! We've agreed that the king should issue the following decree:

For the next thirty days no one is to pray to any god or man except you, O king. Anyone who disobeys will be thrown into the lions' den."

King Darius signed the decree.

Why did the leaders want to get rid of Daniel?

Why didn't
Daniel just stop
praying so he
wouldn't get in
trouble?

When Daniel learned that the decree had been signed and posted, he continued to pray just as he had always done. His house had windows in the upstairs that opened toward Jerusalem. Three times a day he knelt there in prayer, thanking and praising his God.

The leaders came and found him praying, asking God for help. They went straight to the king and said, "Daniel ignores your decree. Three times a day he prays."

At this, the king was very upset and tried his best to get Daniel out of the fix he'd put him in. But then the leaders were back: "Remember, O king, that the king's decree can never be changed."

The king ordered Daniel brought and thrown into the lions' den. But he said to Daniel, "Your God, to whom you are so loyal, is going to get you out of this."

A stone slab was placed over the opening of the den.

The king then went back to his palace. He refused supper. He couldn't sleep. He spent the night fasting.

Why did the king think God would save Daniel?

At daybreak the king got up and hurried to the lions' den. As he approached the den, he called out anxiously, "Daniel, servant of the living God, has your God, whom you serve so loyally, saved you from the lions?"

"O king, live forever!" said Daniel. "My God sent his angel, who closed the mouths of the lions so that they would not hurt me. I've been found innocent before God and also before you, O king. I've done nothing to harm you."

When the king heard these words, he was happy. He ordered Daniel taken up out of the den. When he was hauled up, there wasn't a scratch on him. He had trusted his God.

PRAY

Write down some of the things that scare you. Ask God to help you to not be afraid.

LIVE

Pick a place in your room near a window and spend a few minutes today thanking and praising God like Daniel did.

Role-play the story of Daniel. First act like Daniel and then act like one of the lions who walks around Daniel growling.

JONAH
AND THE HUGE FISH

One day long ago, G๐ᴅ's Word came to Jonah: "Up on your feet and on your way to the big city of Nineveh! Preach to them. They're in a bad way and I can't ignore it any longer."

But instead Jonah got up and went down to the port of Joppa and found a ship headed for Tarshish. He paid the fare and went on board.

Ship to TARSHISH

180

GOD sent a huge storm at sea, the waves towering.

The ship was about to break into pieces. The sailors were terrified. Meanwhile, Jonah had gone down into the hold of the ship to take a nap. He was sound asleep. The captain came to him and said, "Get up! Pray to your god! Maybe your god will see we're in trouble and rescue us."

Then the sailors said to one another, "Let's get to the bottom of this. Let's draw straws to identify who's responsible for this disaster."

So they drew straws. Jonah got the short straw.

Then they asked him: "Why this disaster? Where do you come from?"

He told them, "I'm a Hebrew. I worship GOD, the God of heaven who made sea and land."

At that, the men were frightened, really frightened. As Jonah talked, the sailors realized that he was running away from GOD.

Why did the sailors throw Jonah off the ship?

They said to him, "What are we going to do with you— to get rid of this storm?"

Jonah said, "Throw me overboard, into the sea. Get rid of me and you'll get rid of the storm."

But no. The men tried rowing back to shore. The storm only got worse and worse, wild and raging.

Then they took Jonah and threw him overboard. Immediately the sea was quieted down.

Then God assigned a huge fish to swallow Jonah. Jonah was in the fish's belly three days and nights.

Then Jonah prayed to his God from the belly of the fish. He prayed:

"In trouble, deep trouble, I prayed to God.
He answered me.
I was as far down as a body can go,
Yet you pulled me up from that grave alive,
O God, my God!
When my life was slipping away,
I remembered God,
And my prayer got through to you.
I'm worshiping you, God,
calling out in thanksgiving!
And I'll do what I promised I'd do!"

Then God spoke to the fish, and it vomited up Jonah on the seashore.

PRAY

God sent Jonah to time-out in the belly of a huge fish. Tell God you're sorry for times that you've disobeyed and ask him to help you to be more obedient.

LIVE

Draw and color a big ship, a big fish, and a little Jonah.

Fill up your bathtub and play with a ship, a fish, and a "Jonah" (or use sponges). Act out the Jonah story.

MARY AND ELIZABETH

During the rule of Herod, King of Judea, there was a priest named Zachariah. His wife was named Elizabeth. Together they lived honorably before God, but they were childless and quite old.

It came Zachariah's one turn in life to enter the sanctuary of God in the temple. Unannounced, an angel of God appeared and Zachariah was very afraid.

But the angel reassured him, "Don't fear, Zachariah. Your prayer has been heard. Elizabeth, your wife, will have a son. You are to name him John.

"He'll be filled with the Holy Spirit—he'll get the people ready for God."

It wasn't long before his wife, Elizabeth, became pregnant.

Why was it hard for Zachariah to believe he and his wife would have baby John?

In the sixth month of Elizabeth's pregnancy, God sent the angel Gabriel to the village of Nazareth to a virgin engaged to be married to a man from David's family. His name was Joseph, and the virgin's name, Mary. Upon entering, Gabriel greeted her:

Good morning!

You're beautiful with God's beauty,

Beautiful inside and out!

God be with you.

She was very afraid, but the angel assured her, "Mary, you have nothing to fear. God has a surprise for you: You will become pregnant and give birth to a son and call his name Jesus.

He will be great,

    be called 'Son of the Highest.'

The Lord God will give him

    the throne of his father David."

Mary said to the angel, "But how?"

The angel answered,

If an angel appeared to you and promised something unusual, would you believe him? Why?

The Holy Spirit will come upon you;

Therefore, the child you bring to birth

will be called Holy, Son of God.

"And did you know that your cousin Elizabeth is six months pregnant? Nothing, you see, is impossible with God."

And Mary said,

Yes, I see it all now:

I'm the Lord's maid, ready to serve.

Let it be with me

just as you say.

Then the angel left her.

Mary didn't waste a minute. She got up and traveled to a town in Judah in the hill country, straight to Zachariah's house, and greeted Elizabeth. When Elizabeth heard Mary's greeting, the baby in her womb leaped. She was filled with the Holy Spirit, and sang out exuberantly,

You're so blessed among women,

    and the babe in your womb, also blessed!

And why am I so blessed that

    the mother of my Lord visits me?

The moment the sound of your

    greeting entered my ears,

The babe in my womb

    skipped like a lamb for sheer joy.

Blessed woman, who believed what God said,

    believed every word would come true!

And Mary said,

I'm bursting with God-news;

    I'm dancing the song of my Savior God.

His mercy flows in wave after wave

    on those who are in awe before him.

Mary stayed with Elizabeth for three months and then went back to her own home.

Mary and Elizabeth expected great things. What did they sing about believing God?

When Elizabeth gave birth to a son, her neighbors and relatives celebrated with her.

They were calling him Zachariah after his father. But his mother intervened: "No. He is to be called John."

Then Zachariah was filled with the Holy Spirit and prophesied,

Blessed be the Lord, the God of Israel;

    he came and set his people free.

He set the power of salvation in the center of our lives,

    and in the very house of David his servant.

And you, my child, "Prophet of the Highest,"

    will go ahead of the Master to prepare his ways,

Present the offer of salvation to his people,

    the forgiveness of their sins.

The child grew up, healthy and spirited.

PRAY

Pray Psalm 27:14: Stay with GOD!
Take heart. Don't quit. I'll say it
again: Stay with GOD.

LIVE

Make up a song about some of the
things God has done for you and sing
it to him. Teach it to your family or
friends and have a sing-a-long.

Use stuffed animals and dolls to act
out the birth of John.

LUKE
2

THE BIRTH OF JESUS

About that time everyone had to travel to his own hometown to be counted. So Joseph went from Nazareth up to Bethlehem, David's town, for the **census**. He went with Mary, his fiancée, who was pregnant.

While they were there, she gave birth to a son, her firstborn. She wrapped him in a blanket and laid him in a **manger** because there were no other rooms available.

Census —*When the government tries to count all of the people.*
Manger —*A box or trough where animal feed is kept.*

Jesus was born far away from home, in a stable with animals. What would have happened if they had stopped at your house?

194

There were sheepherders camping in the neighborhood. Suddenly, God's angel stood among them. They were terrified. The angel said, "Don't be afraid. I'm here to announce a great and joyful event that is meant for everybody: A **Savior** has just been born in David's town, a Savior who is **Messiah** and Master. This is what you're to look for: a baby wrapped in a blanket and lying in a manger."

At once the angel was joined by a huge angel choir singing God's praises.

Savior—*A special name for Jesus that reminds us that he came to save people from their sins.*

Messiah—*The unique name for the one God promised to be savior, Jesus.*

Why did God send angels to tell sheepherders, instead of the king or other important people?

As the angel choir withdrew into heaven, the sheepherders talked it over. "Let's get over to Bethlehem as fast as we can and see for ourselves what God has revealed to us." They left, running, and found Mary and Joseph, and the baby lying in the manger. Seeing was believing. They told everyone they met what the angels had said about this child.

Mary kept all these things to herself, holding them dear, deep within herself. The sheepherders returned and let loose, glorifying and praising God for everything they had heard and seen. It turned out exactly the way they'd been told!

If you saw the Baby Jesus, who would you tell? Why?

When the eighth day arrived, the child was named Jesus. His parents took him to the temple in Jerusalem to carry out the rituals of the Law.

In Jerusalem at the time, there was a man, Simeon by name, a good man, a man who lived in the prayerful hope of help for Israel. The Holy Spirit had shown him that he would see the Messiah of God before he died. Led by the Spirit, he entered the Temple. As the parents of the child Jesus brought him in, Simeon took him into his arms and blessed God:

With my own eyes I've seen your salvation;

it's now out in the open for everyone to see:

A God-revealing light to the non-Jewish nations,

and of glory for your people Israel.

Jesus' father and mother were speechless with surprise at these words. Simeon went on to bless them.

When they finished everything required by God in the Law, they returned to Galilee and their own town, Nazareth. There the child grew strong in body and wise in spirit. And the grace of God was on him.

PRAY

Learn some Christmas songs of praise to sing like the angels sang when Jesus was born, and sing them to him: "Hark the Herald Angels Sing" or "Joy to the World."

LIVE

Make some special Christmas cards that tell about Baby Jesus and give them to your friends.

Use a doll and act out the story of Baby Jesus with your family or friends.

How did God make
the birthday of
Jesus special?

THE MAGI

After Jesus was born in Bethlehem village, a band of scholars arrived in Jerusalem from the East. They asked around, "Where can we find the newborn King of the Jews? We observed a star in the eastern sky that signaled his birth."

When word of their search got to King Herod, he was terrified. Herod lost no time. He gathered all the high priests and religion scholars in the city together and asked, "Where is the Messiah supposed to be born?"

They told him, "Bethlehem."

203

Herod then arranged a secret meeting with the scholars from the East. He told them about Bethlehem and said, "Go find this child. Leave no stone unturned. As soon as you find him, send word and I'll join you at once in your worship."

Instructed by the king, they set off. Then the star appeared again, the same star they had seen in the eastern skies. It led them on until it came to the place of the child. They were in the right place! They had arrived at the right time!

How far do you think they followed the star?

They entered the house and saw the child in the arms of Mary, his mother. Overcome, they kneeled and worshiped him. Then they opened their luggage and presented gifts: gold, frankincense, myrrh.

In a dream, they were warned not to report back to Herod. So they worked out another route, left without being seen, and returned to their own country.

PRAY

How hard do you look for God? Do you want to find him? Look for him in creation—in the stars, the sky, or in a baby's smile.

LIVE

Make a list of people in need that you'd like to visit and ask your mom and dad to help you plan to see them soon. Start a family tradition of giving gifts to them each Christmas.

Decorate a box with wrapping paper and begin saving money and small gifts to give away at Christmas.

JESUS IS BAPTIZED

While Jesus was living in the Galilean hills, John, called "the Baptizer," was preaching in the desert country of Judea. His message was simple and plain, like his desert surroundings: "Change your life. God's kingdom is here."

John dressed in a camel-hair robe tied at the waist by a leather strap. He lived on a diet of locusts and wild field honey.

If you saw John, what would you think about him?

208

People poured out of Jerusalem, Judea, and the Jordanian countryside to hear and see him in action. There at the Jordan River those who came to confess their sins were baptized into a changed life.

When John realized that a lot of **Pharisees and Sadducees** were showing up because it was becoming the popular thing to do, he exploded: "What do you think you're doing down here? Do you think a little water on you is going to make any difference? It's your life that must change, not your skin! What counts is your life. Is it green and blossoming? Because if it's deadwood, it goes on the fire.

211

"I'm baptizing you here in the river, turning your old life in for a kingdom life. The real action comes next: The main character in this drama will ignite the kingdom life within you, a fire within you, the Holy Spirit within you, changing you from the inside out. He's going to clean house—make a clean sweep of your lives. He'll place everything true in its proper place before God; everything false he'll put out with the trash to be burned."

Why does God change us from the inside out?

Jesus then appeared, arriving at the Jordan River from Galilee. He wanted John to baptize him. John objected, "I'm the one who needs to be baptized, not *you*!"

But Jesus insisted. "Do it. God's work is coming together right now in this baptism." So John did it.

The moment Jesus came up out of the baptismal waters, the skies opened up and he saw God's Spirit—it looked like a dove—descending and landing on him. And along with the Spirit, a voice: "This is my Son, chosen and marked by my love, delight of my life."

PRAY

Ask Jesus to change you on the inside—in your heart, soul, and mind. Tell God about anything you especially want his help with in your life.

LIVE

Discuss baptism with your family. Has anyone you know been baptized? Where? Who baptized them? What was it like? Why did they get baptized?

Draw a picture of Jesus being baptized by John and the Holy Spirit.

WATER INTO WINE

There was a wedding in the village of Cana in Galilee. Jesus' mother was there. Jesus and his disciples were guests also. When they started running low on wine at the wedding banquet, Jesus' mother told the servants, "Whatever he tells you, do it."

216

Can you guess what happened to the water in the stoneware pots?

ix stoneware water pots were there, used by the Jews for washing. Each held twenty to thirty gallons. Jesus ordered the servants, "Fill the pots with water." And they filled them to the brim.

"Now fill your pitchers and take them to the host," Jesus said, and they did.

When the host tasted the water that had become wine (he didn't know what had just happened but the servants, of course, knew), he called out to the bridegroom, "Everybody I know begins with their finest wines and after the guests have had their fill brings in the cheap stuff. But you've saved the best till now!"

This act in Cana of Galilee was the first sign Jesus gave, the first glimpse of his **glory**. And his disciples believed in him.

PRAY

Jesus is your friend. Talk with him about anything that seems impossible to you.

LIVE

Taste watered-down grape juice and regular grape juice. Can you tell the difference?

Have a snack party of cheese, crackers, and grape juice with your stuffed animals or friends.

THE LORD'S PRAYER

Jesus taught his disciples how to live simply in the loving care of God. He said:

"Be especially careful when you are trying to be good so that you don't make a performance out of it. It might be a good play, but the God who made you won't be applauding.

"When you do something for someone else, don't call attention to yourself. When you help someone out, don't think about how it looks. Just do it—quietly and without a show. That is the way your God, who made you in love, working behind the scenes, helps you out.

"And when you come before God to pray, here's what I want you to do: Find a quiet, secluded place. Just be there as simply and honestly as you can manage. The focus will shift from you to God, and you will begin to sense his **grace**.

"This is your Father you are dealing with, and he knows better than you what you need. With a God like this loving you, you can pray very simply. Like this:

Our Father in heaven,
Reveal who you are.
Set the world right;
Do what's best—
    as above, so below.
Keep us alive with three square meals.
Keep us forgiven with you and forgiving others.
Keep us safe from ourselves and the Devil.
You're in charge!
You can do anything you want!
You're ablaze in beauty!
    Yes. Yes. Yes.

How did Jesus say we should pray?

Grace—*When someone does something special for you that you don't deserve.*

224

"If you decide for God, living a life of God-worship, it follows that you don't fuss about what's on the table at mealtimes or whether the clothes in your closet are in fashion. There is far more to your life than the food you put in your stomach, more to your outer appearance than the clothes you hang on your body. Look at the birds, careless in the care of God. And you count far more to him than birds.

"Has anyone by fussing in front of the mirror ever gotten taller by so much as an inch? All this time and money wasted on fashion—do you think it makes that much difference? Instead of looking at the fashions, walk out into the fields and look at the wildflowers. The ten best-dressed men and women in the country look shabby alongside them.

What things did God say we're not to spend time worrying about?

"If God gives such attention to the appearance of wildflowers—most of which are never even seen—don't you think he'll attend to you, take pride in you, do his best for you? What I'm trying to do here is to get you to relax; you'll find all your everyday human concerns will be met."

PRAY

Pray like Jesus prayed in the Lord's Prayer. Praise God, thank him, and ask him for forgiveness and protection.

LiVE

Secretly clean your room, do the dishes, or put away your toys without being told and without telling anyone you did it.

JESUS CALMS THE SEA

When Jesus saw that a curious crowd was growing by the minute, he told his disciples to take him to the other side of the lake. Then he got in a boat, his disciples with him. The next thing they knew, they were in a severe storm. Waves were crashing into the boat—and Jesus was sound asleep! They woke him, pleading, "Master, save us! We're going down!"

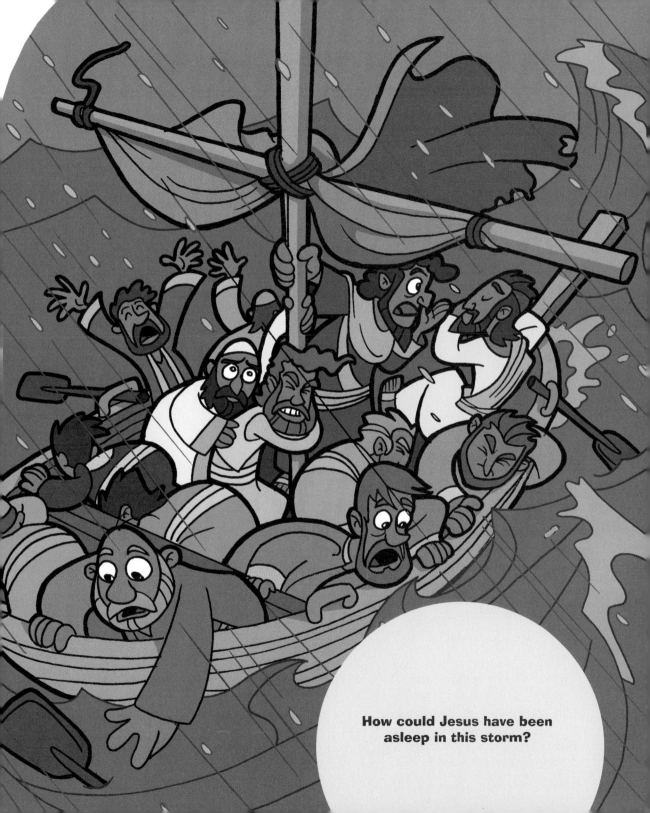

How could Jesus have been
asleep in this storm?

Jesus scolded them. "Why are you such cowards, such faint-hearts?" Then he stood up and told the wind to be silent, the sea to quiet down: "Silence!" The sea became smooth as glass.

The men rubbed their eyes, astonished. "What's going on here? Wind and sea at his command!"

Back in the boat, Jesus and the disciples recrossed the sea to Jesus' hometown. They were hardly out of the boat when some men carried a crippled man on a stretcher and set him down in front of them. Jesus, impressed by their bold belief, said to the crippled man, "Cheer up, son. I forgive your sins." Some religion scholars whispered, "Why, he can't do that!"

How would you feel if you were crippled and Jesus forgave your sins?

Jesus knew what they were thinking, and said, "Why this whispering? Which do you think is simpler: to say, 'I forgive your sins,' or, 'Get up and walk'? Well, just so it's clear that I'm the Son of Man and authorized to do either, or both. . . ." At this he turned to the crippled man and said, "Get up. Take your bed and go home." And the man did it. The crowd was surprised, amazed, and pleased that God had given authority to Jesus to work among them this way.

PRAY

Thank God that he can forgive sins and heal the sick.

LIVE

Make your own storm in a bottle. Take two empty 2-liter plastic pop bottles. Remove the lids and fill one bottle 3/4 full of water. Add a tablespoon of glitter. Tape the empty bottle securely on top of the opening of the full bottle with duct tape. When ready, turn the bottles upside down with the water-filled bottle on top, and swirl fast. Set them on the table and watch the "storm."

BREAD AND FISH FOR ALL

Jesus went across the Sea of Galilee. A huge crowd followed him, attracted by the miracles they had seen him do among the sick. When he got to the other side, he climbed a hill and sat down, surrounded by his disciples. It was nearly time for the Feast of Passover, kept annually by the Jews.

When Jesus looked out and saw that a large crowd had arrived, he said to Philip, "Where can we buy bread to feed these people?" He said this to stretch Philip's faith. He already knew what he was going to do.

Philip answered, "Two hundred silver coins wouldn't be enough to buy bread for each person to get a piece."

How do you think the little boy felt when Jesus fed the people with his lunch?

One of the disciples—it was Andrew, brother to Simon Peter—said, "There's a little boy here who has five barley loaves and two fish. But that's a drop in the bucket for a crowd like this."

Jesus said, "Make the people sit down." There was a nice carpet of green grass in this place. They sat down, about five thousand of them. Then Jesus took the bread and, having given thanks, gave it to those who were seated. He did the same with the fish. All ate as much as they wanted.

When the people had eaten their fill, he said to his disciples, "Gather the leftovers so nothing is wasted." They went to work and filled twelve large baskets with leftovers from the five barley loaves.

PRAY

Talk to God about things that are hard for you to share. Ask him to help you share them with others. Thank him for something special he has given you.

LiVE

Try sharing one cookie by taking turns breaking it in half and in half again. Count how many pieces one cookie makes. Then have a big milk-and-cookie snack.

Decide to share something without being asked this week. Talk about ways your family can share with others.

THE GOOD SAMARITAN

A religion scholar stood up with a question to test Jesus. "Teacher, what do I need to do to get eternal life?"

He answered, "What's written in God's Law? How do you understand it?"

The scholar said, "That you love the Lord your God with all your passion and prayer and muscle and mind—and that you love your neighbor as well as you do yourself."

"Good answer!" said Jesus. "Do it and you'll live."

What do you think
eternal life is?

Looking for a way out, he asked, "And just how would you define 'neighbor'?"

Jesus answered by telling a story. "There was once a man traveling from Jerusalem to Jericho. On the way he was attacked by robbers. They took his clothes, beat him up, and went off leaving him half-dead. Luckily, a priest was on his way down the same road, but when he saw him he moved across to the other side. Then a Levite religious man showed up; he also avoided the injured man.

"A Samaritan traveling the road came on him. When he saw the man's condition, his heart went out to him. He gave him first aid, washing and bandaging his wounds. Then he lifted him onto his donkey, led him to an inn, and made him comfortable. In the morning he took out two silver coins and gave them to the innkeeper, saying, 'Take good care of him. If it costs any more, put it on my bill— I'll pay you on my way back.'

Who is your neighbor?

"What do you think? Which of the three became a neighbor to the man attacked by robbers?"

"The one who treated him kindly," the religion scholar responded.

Jesus said, "Go and do the same."

PRAY

Pray for "neighbors" on your block, in your school, and around the world.

LIVE

Plan with your family to do something for someone who needs help or encouragement.

Bake cookies or a cake to give to a neighbor. Offer to help rake leaves, shovel snow, or sweep the sidewalk.

THE PRODIGAL SON

There was once a man who had two sons. The younger said to his father, "Father, I want right now what's coming to me."

So the father divided the property between them. It wasn't long before the younger son packed his bags and left for a distant country.

Why do you think the son left home with everything his father gave him?

There he wasted everything he had. After he had gone through all his money, there was a bad famine all through that country and he began to hurt. He signed on with a citizen there who assigned him to his fields to feed the pigs. He was so hungry he would have eaten the corncobs in the pig food, but no one would give him any.

That brought him to his senses. He said, "All those farmhands working for my father sit down to three meals a day, and here I am starving to death. I'm going back to my father. I'll say to him, 'Father, I've sinned against God, I've sinned before you; I don't deserve to be called your son. Take me on as a hired hand.'"
He got right up and went home to his father.

Why did the son waste all of the money?

When he was still a long way off, his father saw him. His heart pounding, he ran out, embraced him, and kissed him. The son started his speech:

"Father, I've sinned against God, I've sinned before you; I don't deserve to be called your son ever again."

But the father wasn't listening. He was calling to the servants, "Quick. Bring a clean set of clothes and dress him. Put the family ring on his finger and sandals on his feet. Then get a grain-fed heifer and roast it. We're going to feast! We're going to have a wonderful time! My son is here—given up for dead and now alive! Given up for lost and now found!" And they began to have a wonderful time.

All this time his older son was out in the field. When the day's work was done he came in. As he approached the house, he heard the music and dancing. Calling over one of the houseboys, he asked what was going on. He told him, "Your brother came home. Your father has ordered a feast because he has him home safe and sound."

The father accepted the son just the way he was. Who accepts us just the way we are?

The older brother stalked off in an angry mood and refused to join in. His father came out and tried to talk to him, but he wouldn't listen. The son said, "Look how many years I've stayed here serving you, never giving you one moment of grief, but have you ever thrown a party for me and my friends? Then this son of yours who has thrown away your money shows up and you go all out with a feast!"

His father said, "Son, you don't understand. You're with me all the time, and everything that is mine is yours—but this is a wonderful time, and we had to celebrate. This brother of yours was dead, and he's alive! He was lost, and he's found!"

PRAY

Have you ever been jealous of someone? Ask God to help you love them instead.

LiVE

See if there is a farm or zoo nearby to visit and watch the pigs or other animals being fed.

The next time you have an argument with your brother, sister, or friend, and then make up, have a milk-and-cookies party to celebrate.

SEEDS, LAMPS, AND A HARVEST

Jesus went back to teaching by the sea. A crowd built up to such a great size that he had to get into a boat, using the boat as a pulpit while the people pushed to the water's edge. He taught by using stories, many stories.

"Listen. What do you make of this? A farmer planted seed. As he scattered the seed, some of it fell on the road and birds ate it. Some fell in the gravel; it sprouted quickly but didn't put down roots, so when the sun came up it withered just as quickly. Some fell in the weeds; as it came up, it was strangled among the weeds and nothing came of it. Some fell on good earth and produced a harvest exceeding his wildest dreams.

"Are you listening to this? Really listening?"

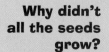

Why didn't all the seeds grow?

259

When they were off by themselves, those who were close to Jesus, along with the Twelve, asked about the stories. He told them, "You've been given insight into God's kingdom. Do you see how this story works? All my stories work this way.

"The farmer plants the Word. Some people are like the seed that falls on the hardened soil of the road. No sooner do they hear the Word than Satan snatches away what has been planted in them.

"And some are like the seed that lands in the gravel. When they first hear the Word, they respond with great enthusiasm. But when the emotions wear off and some difficulty arrives, there is nothing to show for it.

"The seed cast in the weeds represents the ones who hear the kingdom news but are overwhelmed with worries about all the things they have to do and all the things they want to get. The stress strangles what they heard, and nothing comes of it.

"But the seed planted in the good earth represents those who hear the Word, believe it, and produce a harvest beyond their wildest dreams."

Is it OK for us to ask Jesus questions?

Jesus went on: "Does anyone bring a lamp home and put it under a washtub or beneath the bed? Don't you put it up on a table or on the mantel? We're not keeping secrets, we're telling them; we're not hiding things, we're bringing them out into the open.

"Are you listening to this? Really listening?"

How would you feel if the seed you planted died?

Then Jesus said, "God's kingdom is like seed thrown on a field by a man who then goes to bed and forgets about it. The seed sprouts and grows—he has no idea how it happens. The earth does it all without his help: first a green stem of grass, then a bud, then the ripened grain. When the grain is fully formed, he reaps—harvest time!

"How can we picture God's kingdom?
What kind of story can we use? It's like a
pine nut. When it lands on the ground it is quite small
as seeds go, yet once it is planted it grows into a huge
pine tree with thick branches. Eagles nest in it."

With many stories like these, he presented his
message to them. He was never without a story when
he spoke.

PRAY

Obedience is like growing. Ask God to help you be more obedient.

LIVE

Buy a pack of seeds or save some from your fruit or vegetables. Beans or avocado seeds grow easily. Plant them in a pot in a sunny window. Touch the dirt with your finger. When it's dry, water it.

Try the same thing with two pots of seeds. Put one in the sun, and the other in a closet. Talk about what happens to each one.

ZACCHAEUS

Jesus entered and walked through the town of Jericho. There was a man there, his name Zacchaeus, the head tax man and quite rich. He wanted desperately to see Jesus, but the crowd was in his way—he was a short man and couldn't see over the crowd. So he ran on ahead and climbed up in a sycamore tree so he could see Jesus when he came by.

267

When Jesus got to the tree, he looked up and said, "Zacchaeus, hurry down. Today is my day to be a guest in your home."

Zacchaeus scrambled out of the tree, hardly believing his good luck, delighted to take Jesus home with him. Everyone who saw the incident was angry and grumped, "What business does he have getting cozy with this crook?"

Zacchaeus just stood there, a little stunned. He stammered apologetically, "Master, here and now I give away half my income to the poor—and if I'm caught cheating, I pay four times the damages."

Jesus said, "Today is salvation day in this home! Here he is: Zacchaeus, son of Abraham! For the **Son of Man** came to find and restore the lost."

Son of Man—*A special name Jesus gave to himself to emphasize that he was both God and man.*

PRAY

Jesus is like a shepherd searching for lost sheep. Pray for someone you know who doesn't know Jesus. Pray for missionaries who go to help people in other countries.

LIVE

Plan a special dinner and set a place for Jesus at your table. What would you talk about?

Do some tree climbing or try a climbing wall as a family outing.

THE TRIUMPHAL ENTRY AND JESUS IN THE TEMPLE

When they neared Jerusalem, Jesus sent two disciples with these instructions: "Go over to the village across from you. You'll find a donkey there, her colt with her. Untie her and bring them to me. If anyone asks what you're doing, say, 'The Master needs them!' He will send them with you."

Why do you think Jesus didn't ride something fancier, like a chariot?

This is the full story of what was sketched earlier by the prophet:

"Look, your king's on his way,

Riding on a donkey."

The disciples went and did exactly what Jesus told them to do. They led the donkey and colt out, laid some of their clothes on them, and Jesus began to ride. Nearly all the people in the crowd threw their garments down on the road, giving him a royal welcome. Others cut branches from the trees and threw them down as a welcome mat.

Crowds went ahead and crowds followed, all of them calling out,
"**Hosanna** to David's son!" "Blessed is he who comes in God's name!"
"Hosanna in highest heaven!"

As he made his entrance into Jerusalem, the whole city was shaken.
Unnerved, people were asking, "What's going on here? Who is this?"

The parade crowd answered, "This is the prophet Jesus,
the one from Nazareth in Galilee."

What kind of
welcome parade
would people
have for Jesus
today?

Jesus went straight to the Temple and threw out everyone who was buying and selling. He kicked over the tables of dishonest money lenders and the stalls of dove merchants. He quoted this text:

"My house was created a house of prayer;
You have made it a hangout for thieves."

Why was Jesus angry in the Temple?

ow there was room for the blind and crippled to get in. They came to Jesus and he healed them.

When the religious leaders saw the outrageous things he was doing, and heard all the children running and shouting through the Temple, "Hosanna to David's Son!" they were up in arms. "Do you hear what these children are saying?"

Jesus said, "Yes, I hear them. And haven't you read in God's Word, 'From the mouths of children and babies I'll create a place of praise'?"

PRAY

Name some things that make you angry. Ask God to help you control your temper.

LiVE

Gather two or three friends or family members and find some fallen tree branches. Wave them around and shout "Hosanna" to Jesus.

The next time you see someone who is crippled or sick, make the effort to be extra nice to them.

JESUS WASHES THE DISCIPLES' FEET

Just before the Passover Feast, Jesus knew that the time had come to leave this world to go to the Father. Having loved his dear friends, he continued to love them right to the end. It was suppertime. Jesus knew that the Father had put him in complete charge of everything, that he came from God and was on his way back to God. So he got up from the supper table, set aside his robe, and put on an apron. Then he poured water into a basin and began to wash the feet of the disciples, drying them with his apron. When he got to Simon Peter, Peter said, "Master, you wash *my* feet?"

Jesus answered, "You don't understand now what I'm doing, but it will be clear enough to you later."

Peter persisted, "You're not going to wash my feet—ever!"

Jesus said, "If I don't wash you, you can't be part of what I'm doing."

"Master!" said Peter. "Not only my feet, then. Wash my hands! Wash my head!"

Jesus said, "If you've had a bath in the morning, you only need your feet washed now and you're clean from head to toe. My concern, you understand, is **holiness**, not hygiene. So now you're clean." After he had finished washing their feet, he took his robe, put it back on, and went back to his place at the table.

How is holiness like being clean?

Then he said, "Do you understand what I have done to you? You address me as 'Teacher' and 'Master,' and rightly so. That is what I am. So if I, the Master and Teacher, washed your feet, you must now wash each other's feet. I've laid down a pattern for you. What I've done, you do. I'm only pointing out the obvious. A servant is not ranked above his master; an employee doesn't give orders to the employer. If you understand what I'm telling you, act like it—and live a blessed life."

PRAY

Tell God how you feel
about serving others.
Ask him to show you ways
to help people.

LIVE

Have a foot washing like Jesus did.
Get a bowl, soap, and a towel and take
turns washing each other's feet.

Think of special ways to serve
your family this week and do them.

THE LAST SUPPER

Festival of Unleavened Bread—A seven-day celebration that starts with Passover where only flat bread is eaten.

Passover—A special celebration, remembering when God saved the people of Israel from slavery.

On the **Festival of Unleavened Bread**, the disciples came to Jesus and said, "Where do you want us to prepare your **Passover** meal?"

He said, "Enter the city. Go up to a certain man and say, 'The Teacher says, My time is near. I and my disciples plan to celebrate the Passover meal at your house.'" The disciples followed Jesus' instructions to the letter, and prepared the Passover meal.

Why do you think
Jesus wanted
to celebrate the
Passover?

After sunset, he and the Twelve were sitting around the table. During the meal, he said, "I have something hard but important to say to you: One of you is going to hand me over to the men who want to kill me."

They were stunned, and then began to ask, one after another, "It isn't me, is it, Master?"

Jesus answered, "The one who hands me over is someone I eat with daily, one who passes me food at the table. In one sense the Son of Man is going to experience things well-marked by the Scriptures—no surprises here. In another sense that man who turns him in, turns traitor to the Son of Man—better never to have been born than do this!"

Then Judas, already turned traitor, said, "It isn't me, is it, Rabbi?"

Jesus said, "Don't play games with me, Judas."

How did Jesus know who was going to turn him over to the men who wanted to kill him? Who do you think it was?

During the meal, Jesus took and blessed the bread, broke it, and gave it to his disciples:

Take, eat.

This is my body.

Taking the cup and thanking God, he gave it to them:

Drink this, all of you.

This is my blood,

God's new covenant poured out for many people

for the forgiveness of sins.

"I'll not be drinking wine from this cup again until that new day when I'll drink with you in the kingdom of my Father."

They sang a hymn and went directly to Mount Olives.

PRAY

Meditate on what Jesus has done for us and sing a song of praise to him.

LiVE

Memorize 1 Corinthians 11:24: Having given thanks, he broke the bread and said, This is my body, broken for you. Do this to remember me.

Reread the story of the first Passover in Exodus 11–12 and think about why you should remember the things God has done for you.

JESUS' BETRAYAL AND TRIAL

Then Jesus went with them to a garden called Gethsemane and told his disciples, "Stay here while I go over there and pray." Taking along Peter and the two sons of Zebedee, he said, "Stay here and keep watch with me."

Going a little ahead, he fell on his face, praying, "My Father, if there is any way, get me out of this. But please, not what I want. You, what do *you* want?"

When he came back to his disciples, he found them sound asleep. He said to Peter, "Can't you stick it out with me a single hour?"

He then left them a second time. Again he prayed, "My Father, if there is no other way than this, I'm ready. Do it your way."

When he came back, he again found them sound asleep. This time he let them sleep on, and went back a third time to pray.

When he came back the next time, he said, "My time is up, the Son of Man is about to be handed over to the hands of sinners. Get up! Let's get going!"

Do you think
Jesus knew that
Judas was secretly
pointing him out?

The words were barely out of his mouth when
Judas showed up, and with him a gang from the
high priests and religious leaders. Judas had
worked out a sign with them: "The one I kiss,
that's the one—grab him." He went straight to
Jesus, greeted him, and kissed him.

Then they came on him—grabbed him
and roughed him up.

The gang that had grabbed Jesus led him before Caiaphas the Chief Priest.

The Chief Priest said, "I command you by the authority of the living God to say if you are the Messiah, the Son of God."

Jesus answered: "You yourself said it. And that's not all. Soon you'll see it for yourself:

The Son of Man seated at the right hand of the Mighty One,

Arriving on the clouds of heaven."

At that, the Chief Priest lost his temper, ripping his clothes, and yelling.

They all said, "Death! That seals his death sentence."

Who did Jesus agree he was?

Jesus was placed before Pilate, the governor, who questioned him: "Are you the 'King of the Jews'?"

Jesus said, "If you say so."

But when the accusations came from the high priests and religious leaders, he said nothing. Pilate asked him, "Aren't you going to say something?" Jesus kept silence—not a word from his mouth. The governor was impressed, really impressed.

It was an old custom during the Feast for the governor to pardon a single prisoner named by the crowd. At the time, they had the infamous Barabbas in prison. With the crowd before him, Pilate said, "Which prisoner do you want me to pardon: Barabbas, or Jesus the so-called Christ?"

They said, "Barabbas!"

"Then what do I do with Jesus, the so-called Christ?"

They all shouted, "Nail him to a cross!"

Then he pardoned Barabbas. But he had Jesus whipped, and then handed him over for **crucifixion.**

PRAY

Read 1 Peter 2:23: They called him every name in the book and he said nothing back. He suffered in silence, content to let God set things right.

Ask God to help you always say kind things to others.

LIVE

When we follow Jesus, we need to obey God like he did. Talk about what that means with your family.

Make stick figures out of Popsicle sticks and act out the story of Jesus, Pilate, and Barabbas. Who would you set free?

THE CRUCIFIXION

As they led Jesus off, they made Simon, a man from Cyrene who happened to be coming in from the countryside, carry the cross behind Jesus. A huge crowd of people followed, along with women weeping and carrying on.

Two others, both criminals, were taken along with him for execution.

When they got to the place called Skull Hill, they crucified him, along with the criminals, one on his right, the other on his left.

Jesus prayed, "Father, forgive them; they don't know what they're doing."

The people stood there staring at Jesus, and the ringleaders made faces, teasing, "He saved others. Let's see him save himself! The Messiah of God—ha! The Chosen—ha!"

The soldiers also came up and poked fun at him, making a game of it: "So you're King of the Jews! Save yourself!"

Printed over him was a sign: THIS IS THE KING OF THE JEWS.

What did Jesus ask God to do to the soldiers and others who hurt and killed him?

One of the criminals hanging alongside cursed him: "Some Messiah you are! Save yourself! Save us!"

But the other one made him quiet down: "Have you no fear of God? We deserve this, but not him—he did nothing to deserve this."

Then he said, "Jesus, remember me when you enter your kingdom."

He said, "Don't worry, I will. Today you will join me in paradise."

What did the criminal on the other cross do in order to go to heaven with Jesus?

By now it was noon. The whole earth became dark, the darkness lasting three hours—a total blackout. Jesus called loudly, "Father, I place my life in your hands!" Then he breathed his last. When the captain there saw what happened, he honored God: "This man was innocent! A good man, and innocent!"

All who had come around to watch were overcome with grief and headed home. Those who knew Jesus well, along with the women who had followed him from Galilee, stood at a respectful distance and kept watch.

After watching Jesus die, what did the captain of the soldiers say about him?

There was a man by the name of Joseph, a member of the Jewish High Council, a man of good heart and good character. He had not gone along with the plans and actions of the council. He went to Pilate and asked for the body of Jesus. Taking him down from the cross, he wrapped him in a linen covering and placed him in a tomb chiseled into the rock, a tomb never yet used. The Sabbath was just about to begin.

The women who had been companions of Jesus from Galilee followed along. They saw the tomb where Jesus' body was placed. Then they went back to prepare burial spices and perfumes. They rested quietly on the Sabbath, as commanded.

PRAY

Have you done anything that you are sorry about? You can always talk to Jesus and ask him to forgive you because he loves you.

LIVE

Build three crosses out of Popsicle sticks, one for each of the criminals and one for Jesus. Stick them in a mound of dirt to remember Jesus' death on the cross.

Sit in a circle with your mom and dad and take turns teasing each other. Then talk about how Jesus felt when everyone made fun of him.

THE RESURRECTION

Early in the morning on the first day of the week, while it was still dark, Mary Magdalene came to the tomb and saw that the stone was moved away from the entrance. She ran at once to Simon Peter and the other disciple, breathlessly panting, "They took the Master from the tomb. We don't know where they've put him."

Why was Mary upset at the tomb?

Peter and the other disciple ran, neck and neck. The other disciple got to the tomb first, outrunning Peter. Stooping to look in, he saw the pieces of linen cloth lying there. Simon Peter arrived after him, entered the tomb, and observed the linen cloths lying there. Then the other disciple, the one who had gotten there first, went into the tomb, took one look at the linen cloths, and believed. The disciples then went back home.

But Mary stood outside the tomb weeping. As she wept, she knelt to look into the tomb and saw two angels sitting there, at the head and at the foot of where Jesus' body had been laid. They said to her, "Woman, why do you weep?"

"They took my Master," she said, "and I don't know where they put him." After she said this, she turned away and saw Jesus standing there. But she didn't recognize him.

Jesus spoke to her, "Woman, why do you weep? Who are you looking for?"

She, thinking that he was the gardener, said, "Mister, if you took him, tell me where you put him so I can care for him."

Jesus said, "Mary."

Turning to face him, she said, "Teacher!"

Jesus said, "Go to my brothers and tell them, 'I ascend to my Father and your Father, my God and your God.'"

Later on that day, the disciples had gathered together, but, fearful of the Jews, had locked all the doors in the house. Jesus entered, stood among them, and said, "Peace to you."

But Thomas, one of the Twelve, was not with them when Jesus came. The other disciples told him, "We saw the Master."

But he said, "Unless I see the nail holes in his hands, put my finger in the nail holes, and stick my hand in his side, I won't believe it."

Eight days later, his disciples were again in the room. This time Thomas was with them. Jesus came through the locked doors, stood among them, and said, "Peace to you."

Then he focused his attention on Thomas. "Take your finger and examine my hands. Take your hand and stick it in my side. Don't be unbelieving. Believe."

Thomas said, "My Master! My God!"

Jesus said, "So, you believe because you've seen with your own eyes. Even better blessings are in store for those who believe without seeing."

PRAY

Jesus loves you very much, enough to die on a cross for you. Think of some special things to thank Jesus for.

LIVE

Borrow a few socks from your mom or dad. Put one object or toy in each sock and tie a knot in the end. Take turns guessing what the object is. Talk with your parents about what it means to believe in God even though you can't see him.

Make a tomb out of clay and find a stone to put over the entrance. Play-act the Resurrection story with your family or friends.

JESUS GOES TO HEAVEN

This is the story of everything that Jesus began to do and teach until the day he said good-bye to the apostles, the ones he had chosen through the Holy Spirit, and was taken up to heaven. After his death, he presented himself alive to them in many different settings over a period of forty days. In face-to-face meetings, he talked to them about things concerning the kingdom of God. As they met and ate meals together, he told them that they were not to leave Jerusalem but "wait for what the Father promised: you will be baptized in the Holy Spirit. And soon."

How far do you
think the ends of
the world are?

When they were together for the last time they asked, "Master, are you going to bring back the **kingdom** to Israel now? Is this the time?"

He told them, "You don't get to know the time. Timing is the Father's business. What you'll get is the Holy Spirit. And when the Holy Spirit comes on you, you will be able to be my witnesses in Jerusalem, all over Judea and Samaria, even to the ends of the world."

These were his last words. As they watched, he was taken up and disappeared in a cloud. They stood there, staring into the empty sky. Suddenly two men appeared—in white robes! They said, "You Galileans!—why do you just stand here looking up at an empty sky? This very Jesus who was taken up from among you to heaven will come as certainly—and mysteriously—as he left."

Kingdom —*The place where God is King.*

So they left the mountain called Olives and returned to Jerusalem. It was a little over half a mile. They went to the upper room they had been using as a meeting place:

Peter, John, James, Andrew, Philip, Thomas, Bartholomew, Matthew, James, son of Alphaeus, Simon the Zealot, Judas, son of James.

They agreed they were in this for good, completely together in prayer, the women included. Also Jesus' mother, Mary, and his brothers.

PRAY

Talk to God about people who don't know about Jesus. Do you have a friend or family member you want to pray for?

LIVE

Write down the important things people need to know about Jesus. Think of some ways you could "go to the ends of the world" and tell people about Jesus.

Invite a student from a different country to dinner or be a pen pal.

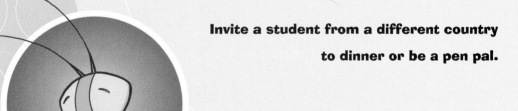

Feast of Pentecost—A festival in Israel where people gave thanks to God for a successful grain harvest.

PENTECOST

When the **Feast of Pentecost** came, the believers were all together in one place. Without warning there was a sound like a strong wind— no one could tell where it came from. It filled the whole building. Then, like a wildfire, the Holy Spirit spread through the people, and they started speaking in a number of different languages as the Spirit prompted them.

What would your friends and family think if you suddenly spoke in another language?

There were many Jews staying in Jerusalem just then, devout pilgrims from all over the world. When they heard the sound, they came on the run. Then when they heard, one after another, their own mother tongues being spoken, they were amazed. They couldn't for the life of them figure out what was going on, and kept saying, "Aren't these all Galileans? How come we're hearing them talk in our various mother tongues?

"They're speaking our languages, describing God's mighty works!

"What's going on here?"

Why could the pilgrims understand the different languages spoken?

That's when Peter stood up and, backed by the other eleven, spoke out with bold urgency: "Fellow Jews, all of you who are visiting Jerusalem, listen carefully and get this story straight. This is what the prophet Joel announced would happen:

"In the Last Days," God says, "I'll pour out my Spirit on those who serve me, men and women both, and they'll **prophesy**."

"Fellow Israelites, listen carefully to these words: Jesus the Nazarene, a man sent by God to you, was betrayed by men who took the law into their own hands, and was handed over to you. And you pinned him to a cross and killed him. But God untied the death ropes and raised him up. Death was no match for him. This Jesus, God raised up. And every one of us here is a witness to it. Then, receiving the promise of the Holy Spirit from the Father, he poured out the Spirit he had just received. That is what you see and hear.

"All Israel, then, know this: There's no longer room for doubt—God made him Master and Messiah, this Jesus whom you killed on a cross."

Those who were there listening asked Peter and the other apostles, "Brothers! Brothers! So now what do we do?"

Peter said, "Change your life. Turn to God and be baptized, each of you, in the name of Jesus Christ, so your sins are forgiven. Receive the gift of the Holy Spirit."

What did Peter tell the people to do?

That day about three thousand took him at his word, were baptized and were signed up. And all the believers lived in wonderful harmony, holding everything in common.

They followed a daily discipline of worship in the Temple followed by meals at home, every meal a celebration, exuberant and joyful, as they praised God. People in general liked what they saw. Every day their number grew as God added those who were saved.

PRAY

Ask God to help you get along with your friends and family ("live in harmony") like the disciples did.

LIVE

Have a pretend baptism. Fill a sink with water and baptize your dolls or action figures.

Talk to your mom and dad or Sunday school teacher about being baptized yourself.

How long had the crippled man been unable to walk?

PETER AND JOHN HEAL

One day at three o'clock in the afternoon, Peter and John were on their way into the Temple for a prayer meeting. At the same time there was a man crippled from birth being carried up. Every day he was set down at the Temple gate, the one named Beautiful, to beg from those going into the Temple. When he saw Peter and John about to enter the Temple, he asked for a handout.

What would it be like to see someone dance after not being able to walk for so long?

Peter, with John at his side, looked him straight in the eye and said, "Look here." He looked up, expecting to get something from them.

Peter said, "I don't have a nickel to my name, but what I do have, I give you: In the name of Jesus Christ of Nazareth, walk!" He grabbed him by the right hand and pulled him up. In an instant his feet and ankles became firm. He jumped to his feet and walked.

The man went into the Temple with them, walking back and forth, dancing and praising God. Everybody there saw him walking around and praising God. They recognized him as the one who sat begging at the Temple's Gate Beautiful and rubbed their eyes, astonished, scarcely believing what they were seeing.

The man threw his arms around Peter and John. All the people ran up to where they were at Solomon's Porch to see it for themselves.

When Peter saw he had a congregation, he addressed the people:

"Oh, Israelites, why does this take you by such complete surprise, and why stare at us as if *our* power made him walk? The God of Abraham and Isaac and Jacob, the God of our ancestors, has glorified his Son Jesus. Faith in Jesus' name put this man, whose condition you know so well, on his feet—yes, faith and nothing but faith put this man healed and whole right before your eyes."

PRAY

Peter had no money but he gave the crippled man something better. He prayed for him. Pray for people you know who need help, healing, or encouragement.

LIVE

Ask your parents to take you to a hospital or nursing home to visit the people there.

Hold hands in a circle with your parents or friends. Dance and sing a song of praise.

SAUL ON THE ROAD TO DAMASCUS

All this time Saul, an enemy of the believers, was breathing down the necks of the Master's disciples, out for the kill. He went to the Chief Priest and got arrest warrants to take to the meeting places in Damascus so that if he found anyone there belonging to the Way, whether men or women, he could arrest them and bring them to Jerusalem.

Who did Saul want to put in jail?

339

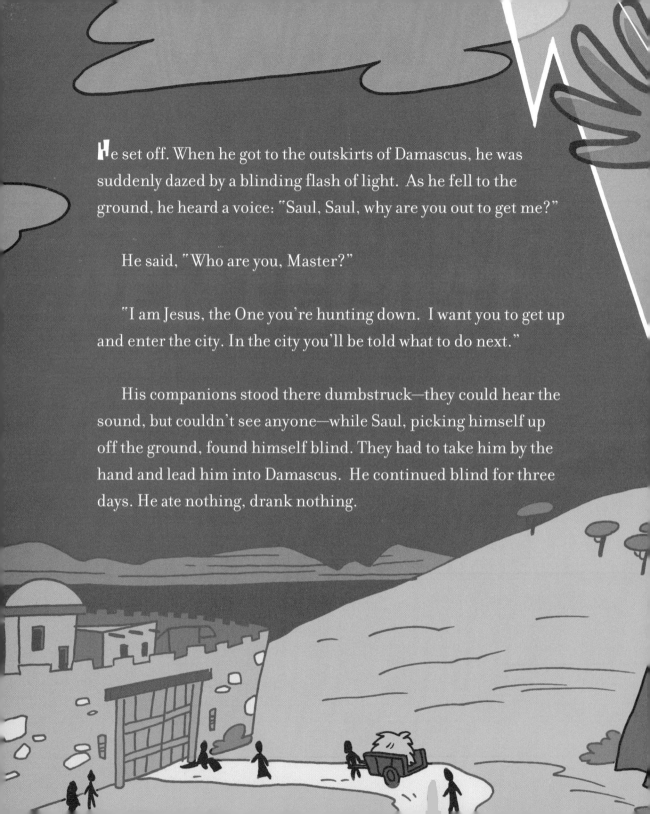

He set off. When he got to the outskirts of Damascus, he was suddenly dazed by a blinding flash of light. As he fell to the ground, he heard a voice: "Saul, Saul, why are you out to get me?"

He said, "Who are you, Master?"

"I am Jesus, the One you're hunting down. I want you to get up and enter the city. In the city you'll be told what to do next."

His companions stood there dumbstruck—they could hear the sound, but couldn't see anyone—while Saul, picking himself up off the ground, found himself blind. They had to take him by the hand and lead him into Damascus. He continued blind for three days. He ate nothing, drank nothing.

How did Jesus get Saul's attention?

There was a disciple in Damascus by the name of Ananias. The Master spoke to him in a vision: "Ananias."

"Yes, Master?" he answered.

"Get up and go over to Straight Avenue. Ask at the house of Judas for a man from Tarsus. His name is Saul. He's there praying. He has just had a dream in which he saw a man named Ananias enter the house and lay hands on him so he could see again."

Ananias protested, "Master, you can't be serious. Everybody's talking about this man and the terrible things he's been doing! And now he's shown up here with papers from the Chief Priest that give him license to do the same to us."

But the Master said, "Don't argue. Go! I have picked him as my personal representative to Gentiles and kings and Jews."

So Ananias went and found the house, placed his hands on blind Saul, and said, "Brother Saul, the Master sent me, the same Jesus you saw on your way here. He sent me so you could see again and be filled with the Holy Spirit." No sooner were the words out of his mouth than something like scales fell from Saul's eyes—he could see again! He got to his feet, was baptized, and sat down with them to a hearty meal.

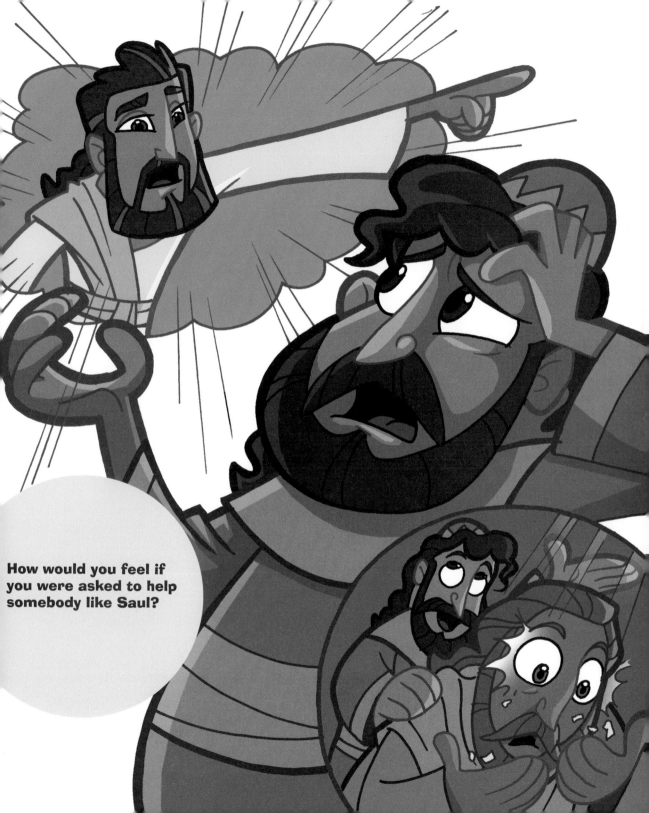

Saul spent a few days getting acquainted with the Damascus disciples, but then went right to work, wasting no time, preaching in the meeting places that this Jesus was the Son of God.

PRAY

Do you know someone who is mean to others? Pray for that person.

LiVE

Take turns walking blindfolded with someone you trust to lead you around.

Draw a picture of the old Saul (angry), and then draw a picture of the new Saul (happier).

Why did King Herod
want to kill Peter?

PETER IS FREED FROM JAIL

ACTS 12

The ruler of Israel, King Herod, got it into his head to go after some of the church members. He arrested Peter and had him thrown in jail, putting four squads of four soldiers each to guard him. He was planning to kill Peter after Passover.

All the time that Peter was under heavy guard in the jailhouse, the church prayed for him continuously.

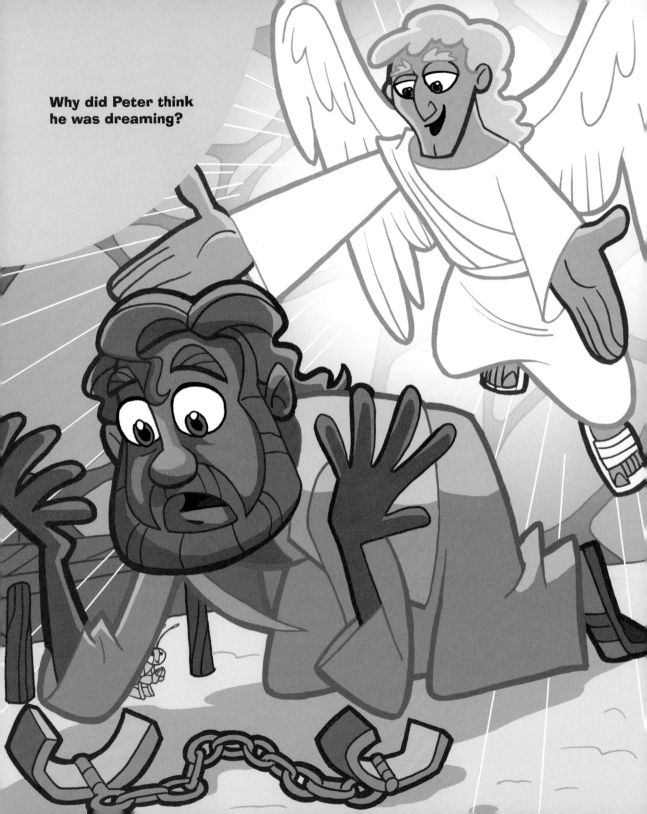

Why did Peter think he was dreaming?

Then the time came for Herod to complete his plan to kill Peter. That night, even though shackled to two soldiers, one on either side, Peter slept like a baby. And there were guards at the door keeping their eyes on the place. Herod was taking no chances!

Suddenly there was an angel at Peter's side and light flooding the room. The angel shook Peter and got him up: "Hurry!" The handcuffs fell off his wrists. The angel said, "Get dressed. Put on your shoes." Peter did it. Then, "Grab your coat and let's get out of here." Peter followed him, but didn't believe it was really an angel—he thought he was dreaming.

Past the first guard and then the second, they came to the iron gate that led into the city. It swung open before them on its own, and they were out on the street, free as the breeze. That's when Peter realized it was no dream. "I can't believe it—this really happened! The Master sent his angel and rescued me from Herod and the Jewish mob."

How would you feel if somebody you thought was in jail suddenly appeared at your front door?

Still shaking his head, amazed, he went to Mary's house, the Mary who was John Mark's mother. The house was packed with praying friends. When he knocked on the door to the courtyard, a young woman named Rhoda came to see who it was. But when she recognized his voice—Peter's voice!—she was so excited and eager to tell everyone Peter was there that she forgot to open the door and left him standing in the street.

But they wouldn't believe her. "You're crazy," they said. She stuck by her story, insisting. They still wouldn't believe her and said, "It must be his angel." All this time poor Peter was standing out in the street, knocking away.

Finally they opened up and saw him—and went wild! Peter put his hands up and calmed them down. He described how the Master had gotten him out of jail.

PRAY

There are Christians in other countries who are in jail today for following Jesus. Ask God to keep them safe, healthy, and encouraged.

LIVE

Put on a family play. Arrest someone for reading the Bible or telling people about Jesus. Pray for them. Have an angel free them from prison.

See if you can find information or books about Christians in prison for their faith.

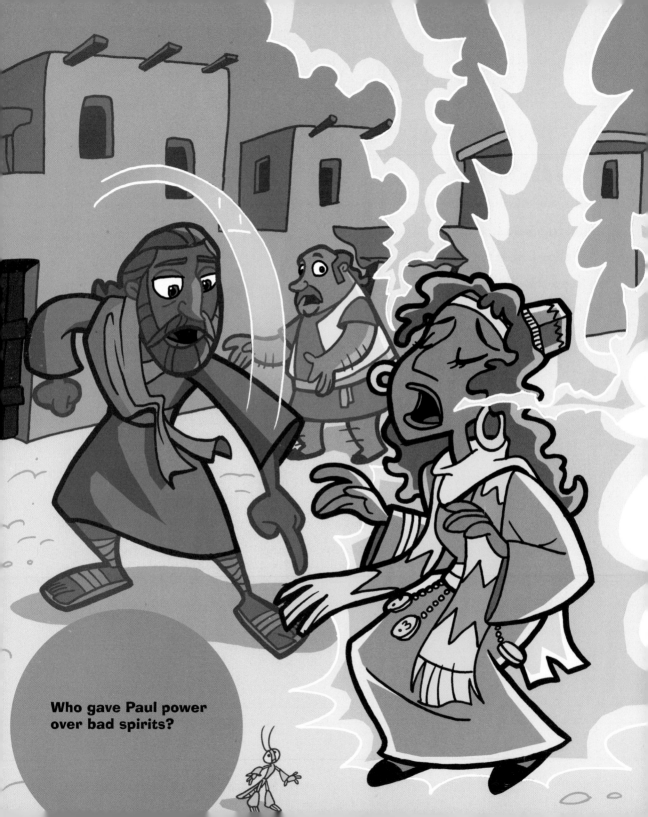

Who gave Paul power over bad spirits?

THE JAILER BECOMES A CHRISTIAN

ACTS 16

One day, on the way to the place of prayer, a slave girl ran into Paul and Silas. She was a fortuneteller and made a lot of money for the people who owned her. She started following Paul around, calling everyone's attention to him by yelling out, "These men are working for the Most High God." She did this for a number of days until Paul, finally fed up with her, turned and commanded the spirit that possessed her, "Out! In the name of Jesus Christ, get out of her!" And it was gone, just like that.

Did Paul and Silas deserve a beating and prison? Why or why not?

When her owners saw that their fortunetelling business was suddenly gone, they went after Paul and Silas, roughed them up and dragged them into the market square. Then the police arrested them and pulled them into a court.

The judges had Paul and Silas's clothes ripped off and ordered a public beating. After beating them black-and-blue, they threw them into jail, telling the jailkeeper to put them under heavy guard so there would be no chance of escape.

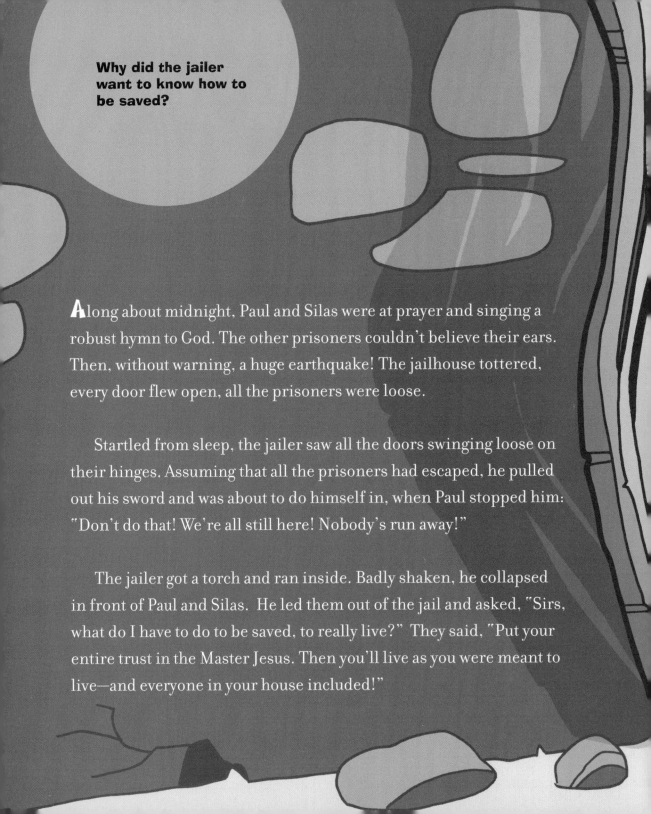

Why did the jailer want to know how to be saved?

Along about midnight, Paul and Silas were at prayer and singing a robust hymn to God. The other prisoners couldn't believe their ears. Then, without warning, a huge earthquake! The jailhouse tottered, every door flew open, all the prisoners were loose.

Startled from sleep, the jailer saw all the doors swinging loose on their hinges. Assuming that all the prisoners had escaped, he pulled out his sword and was about to do himself in, when Paul stopped him: "Don't do that! We're all still here! Nobody's run away!"

The jailer got a torch and ran inside. Badly shaken, he collapsed in front of Paul and Silas. He led them out of the jail and asked, "Sirs, what do I have to do to be saved, to really live?" They said, "Put your entire trust in the Master Jesus. Then you'll live as you were meant to live—and everyone in your house included!"

They went on to spell out in detail the story of the Master—the entire family got in on this part. They never did get to bed that night. The jailer made them feel at home, dressed their wounds, and then—he couldn't wait till morning!—was baptized, he and everyone in his family. There in his home, he had food set out for a festive meal. It was a night to remember: He and his entire family had put their trust in God; everyone in the house was in on the celebration.

PRAY

Can you think of anyone who needs to know that Jesus loves them? Talk with God about them.

LIVE

Play a game of hide-and-seek. The seeker is the jailer. The jailer counts to 20 while the others hide. When done counting, the jailer calls out, "Paul and Silas! Where are you?" The first person to be found becomes the next jailer.

Build a jail out of pillows, chairs, and blankets. Get inside of it and then count how long it takes you to escape. Have a pretend earthquake to escape from jail.

1 CORINTHIANS 13

LOVE is the BEST

If I speak with beautiful words and the joy of angels but don't love, I'm nothing but the creaking of a rusty gate.

Can you make an ugly noise like a creaking gate?

If I speak God's Word with power, revealing all his mysteries and making everything plain as day, and if I have faith that says to a mountain, "Jump," and it jumps, but I don't love, I'm nothing.

If I give everything I own to the poor and even go to the stake to be burned as a martyr, but I don't love, I've gotten nowhere. So, no matter what I say, what I believe, and what I do, I'm penniless without love.

What is the main thing God wants us to do?

Love never gives up.

Love cares more for others than for self.

Love doesn't want what it doesn't have.

Love doesn't strut,

Doesn't have a swelled head,

Doesn't force itself on others,

Isn't always "me first,"

Doesn't fly off the handle,

Doesn't keep score of the sins of others,

Doesn't celebrate when others are down,

Takes pleasure in the revelation of truth,

Puts up with anything,

Trusts God always,

Always looks for the best,

Never looks back,

But keeps going to the end.

How do you feel when you love someone?

Love never dies. We know only a portion of the truth, and what we say about God is always incomplete.

We don't yet see things clearly. We're squinting in a fog, peering through a mist. But it won't be long before the weather clears and the sun shines bright! We'll see it all then, see it all as clearly as God sees us, knowing him directly just as he knows us!

But for right now, until that time, we have three things to do: Trust steadily in God, hope unswervingly, love extravagantly. And the best of the three is love.

PRAY

Think of people you see every week, including your family. Ask God to help you be a more loving person to them.

LIVE

If not loving sounds like a rusty gate, try to think of three nice sounds that love might sound like.

This week, try to say "I love you" to someone every day.

HUMBLE YOURSELF

If you've gotten anything at all out of following Christ, if his love has made any difference in your life, if being in a community of the Spirit means anything to you, if you have a heart, if you *care*— then do me a favor: Agree with each other, love each other, be deep-spirited friends. Don't push your way to the front; don't sweet-talk your way to the top. Put yourself aside, and help others get ahead. Don't be obsessed with getting your own way. Forget yourselves long enough to lend a helping hand.

370

How does love
make a difference
in your life?

What would you do if you were to follow Christ's example of how to live?

Think of yourselves the way Christ Jesus thought of himself. He had equal status with God but didn't think so much of himself that he had to cling to the advantages of that status no matter what. Not at all. When the time came, he set aside the privileges of being God and took on the status of a slave, became *human*! Having become human, he stayed human. It was an incredibly humbling process. He didn't claim special privileges. Instead, he lived a selfless, obedient life and then died a selfless, obedient death—and the worst kind of death at that: a crucifixion.

Because of that obedience, God lifted him high and honored him far beyond anyone or anything, ever, so that all created beings in heaven and on earth—even those long ago dead and buried—will bow in worship before this Jesus Christ, and call out in praise that he is the Master of all, to the glorious honor of God the Father.

PRAY

Think of ways you can humble yourself and put others first. Ask God to help you act unselfishly.

LIVE

Play a game of "Simon Says." Whatever "Simon" says, everyone has to do it. If you do something and "Simon" doesn't say or order it, you sit down. See who's standing longest. Talk about what it means to do what Jesus says.

Sometime this week, serve your friends or family a snack, and clean up by yourself. Practice being unselfish.

HEAVEN

ohn, one of Jesus' disciples, received this vision from an angel: I saw Heaven and earth new-created. Gone the first Heaven, gone the first earth, gone the sea.

I saw Holy Jerusalem, new-created, descending out of Heaven, as ready for God as a bride for her husband.

I heard a voice thunder from the Throne: "Look! Look! God has moved into the neighborhood, making his home with men and women! They're his people, he's their God. He'll wipe every tear from their eyes. Death is gone for good—tears gone, crying gone, pain gone—all the first order of things gone."

How is Heaven different from earth?

One of the Seven Angels spoke to me: "Come here. I'll show you the Bride, the Wife of the Lamb." He took me away in the Spirit to an enormous, high mountain and showed me Holy Jerusalem descending out of Heaven from God.

The City shimmered like a precious gem, light-filled, pulsing light. She had a wall majestic and high with twelve gates. At each gate stood an Angel.

The wall was jasper, the color of Glory, and the City was pure gold, clear as glass. The foundations of the City walls were garnished with every precious gem imaginable. The twelve gates were twelve pearls, each gate a single pearl.

What do you like most about Heaven?

Can you name some things not found in Heaven?

The main street of the City was pure gold, clear as glass. But there was no sign of a Temple, for the Lord God—the Sovereign-Strong—and the Lamb are the Temple. The City doesn't need sun or moon for light. God's Glory is its light, the Lamb its lamp! Its gates will never be shut by day, and there won't be any night. They'll bring the glory and honor of the nations into the City. Nothing and no one dirty will get into the City. Only those whose names are written in the Lamb's Book of Life will get in.

Then the Angel showed me Water-of-Life River, crystal bright. It flowed from the Throne of God and the Lamb, right down the middle of the street. The Tree of Life was planted on each side of the River, producing twelve kinds of fruit, a ripe fruit each month.

The Throne of God and of the Lamb is at the center. His servants will offer God service—worshiping, they'll look on his face, their foreheads mirroring God. Never again will there be any night. No one will need lamplight or sunlight. The shining of God, the Master, is all the light anyone needs. And they will rule with him age after age after age.

PRAY

God made Heaven a wonderful place for us. Thank him for giving you the chance to go there.

LIVE

Draw a picture of what you think Heaven might look like.

Go outside, lie on your back in the grass, and look up at the sky. Now close your eyes and try to imagine Heaven way past what you can see.

Eugene H. Peterson is a pastor, scholar, writer, and poet. After teaching at a seminary and then giving nearly thirty years to church ministry in the Baltimore area, he created *The Message*—a vibrant Bible translation that connects with today's readers like no other. It took Peterson a full ten years to complete. He worked from the original Greek and Hebrew texts to guarantee authenticity. At the same time, his ear was always tuned to the cadence and energy of contemporary English. Eugene and his wife, Jan, now live in his native Montana. They are the parents of three and the grandparents of six.

Rob Corley and Tom Bancroft have over thirty years of combined experience in the animation industry, most of which was for Walt Disney Feature animation. While at Disney, the partners had the opportunity to contribute animation on ten animated feature films, five animated shorts, and numerous special projects and commercials. Some of the classic films include *Beauty and the Beast*, *The Lion King*, *Aladdin*, *Mulan*, *Lilo and Stitch*, and *Brother Bear*. Bancroft was also a character designer and director for Big Idea Productions, makers of the family-friendly *Veggie Tales* video series.

They are partners in Funnypages Productions, LLC, a company that provides illustration, character design, and artistic animation development. Funnypages Productions has also developed many original properties for film and television and illustrated over twenty-five children's books. They and their families live in Nashville, Tennessee. For more information, see www.funnypagesprod.com.